CHILDHOOD ANTIQUES

CHILDHOOD ANTIQUES

James Mackay

Taplinger Publishing Company
New York

First published in the United States in 1976 by
TAPLINGER PUBLISHING CO., INC.
    New York, New York
Copyright © 1976 by James Mackay
    All rights reserved.
    Printed in Italy.

Library of Congress Catalog Card
Number: 76-11668
ISBN 0-8008-1442-8

Published in Great Britain by
Ward Lock Limited, London

CONTENTS

Introduction

The Victorian era was the heyday of the nursery. Of course, the higher levels of society in every age, before and since, had things organized in such a manner that they were occupied as little as possible with the rearing of their young. In the extended family system of many primitive communities there was no shortage of elderly aunts and grandmothers to shoulder the main burden of child-rearing while both parents worked; and even to this day we have a dual system represented at the ends of the social spectrum by the au pair and the child-minder. Shortage and comparative expense of domestic labour, together with the rise of the crèche, the kindergarten and the pre-school playgroup, have led to a marked decline in the nursery, though it still exists among the wealthiest classes.

The decline in infant mortality and the marked increase in population attendant on the Industrial Revolution resulted in the typical Victorian family. The Queen herself had nine children and Charles Dickens had ten. Families of twelve or even sixteen children were not uncommon. A woman marrying in her mid-twenties could continue to bear children into her late forties and be involved (to a greater or lesser degree) with their upbringing until her late fifties or early sixties. Long before the dawn of women's suffrage, let alone women's lib, the more affluent families had solved this problem to their own satisfaction. Not only the upper classes—royalty, the aristocracy and the landed gentry—but the so-called middle classes managed to remove as much of the burden of child-rearing as possible from the parents by the employment of nurses and nannies. Low taxation and a comparatively low cost of living enabled even quite modestly paid white-collar workers to maintain a household which would include one or more domestic servants. Building costs were likewise low by present-day standards, and one has only to look at the solid rows of terraces in the London suburbs from Sydenham to Ealing, for example, to appreciate that clerks in City offices and skilled artisans alike could keep their large families in some style.

The period from 1870 to the eve of the First World War may be regarded as the Golden Age of the middle classes—not only in Britain, but in western Europe and North America as well. The rapid development of industry and international commerce in France, Germany and Italy in this period paralleled the developments in England, and millions joined the ranks of the new bourgeoisie. The raising of standards of living, however, was at its most dramatic in the United States between the end of the Civil War in 1865 and the end of the century. By 1890 the population had risen to fifty million and industrial expansion proceeded at a meteoric pace. A combination of inventiveness and commercial acumen made the United States the world's leading trading nation by the turn of the century. A third of the nation might still be below the poverty line in 1900, but the majority of the population, even then, enjoyed a much higher standard of living than their European counterparts. The life of the middle-class child in America was little different from that of children in Victorian England or the Kaiser's Germany. Life in New England differed in no material sense from that of the Old World; parental authority could be just as strict and remote. Lower down in the social scale, however, and further west than the eastern seaboard, family life tended to be more integrated and the nursery was not so much a world of its own.

There were great extremes of wealth and poverty in Victorian times, and a large proportion of the population lived in conditions of unbelievable squalor. But for those who belonged to the 'respectable' classes, life had an element of spaciousness, leisure and grandeur that is almost entirely absent today. Sixty years of social legislation and latterly the Welfare State have levelled British society and removed the extremes; and the same is true of society in the USA, Canada and other countries of the western world. There are those who look back nostalgically at Victorian and Edwardian times as a period of peace and prosperity, and regard the nursery of that period as a cosy haven of childhood. There are others, however, who appreciate that it was a period of immense inequality and injustice in many respects, and who would regard the Victorian nursery as a prison all too often dominated by the ignorance and tyranny of ill-educated nannies. The truth, in both instances, probably lies somewhere in the middle. At any rate, whether one has any real or imagined memory of the Victorian nursery, the dimly recollected elements in one's own childhood and infancy are usually pleasurable rather than unpleasant.

Of all the collecting fields nursery antiques is probably the most attractive and appealing, particularly to a generation where childhood coincided with the austere years of the Second World War and its aftermath. To those collectors the toys, dolls, games and impedimenta of the old-style nursery have an opulence, elegance and charm which are largely absent from their post-war counterparts. To an older generation of collectors these things are a poignant reminder of their own childhood. Nostalgia obviously plays an important part. It requires very little imagination to identify with the long forgotten owners of nursery antiques; this charm of association with the children of yesteryear is seldom so strong in the inanimate objects from the adult world of the past.

The cynics remark that even nostalgia is not what it used to be; but with regard to the nursery it is still a very powerful emotion. Whether the motive is nostalgia or just plain infantile regression, there is no doubt that the toys and dolls, games and pastimes, the literature, clothing and furniture pertaining to the childhood of yesteryear possess enormous appeal for the collector. Their smallness compared to other forms of antiques is an added recommendation.

For all practical purposes the term 'antique' has now been redefined to include any artefact produced up to 1930—a date which accords most conveniently with the decline of the old-fashioned nursery in the strict sense. Most collectors, however, would be reasonably flexible in interpreting the word 'antique' and include collectables of more recent vintage. This applies to many fields of collecting, but it is particularly valid in considering the mementoes of childhood. Games lose their pieces, books become dog-eared and torn, and toys are all too easily broken. Bearing in mind the careless and rough usage inflicted on such things by their youthful owners, it is a miracle that so much has survived from the nursery of yesteryear. Indeed, the astute collector is probably the one who is studying the catalogues of contemporary retailers and manufacturers and purchasing the items that will acquire an antiquarian interest in the future.

Church bazaars, fairs and jumble sales, up to ten years ago, used to be a happy hunting ground for nursery memorabilia. Nowadays jumble sales tend to mirror the instant obsolescence of the affluent society and seldom yield much that is truly antique, but none the less this is a source of material that should never be overlooked. Inevitably interest in things that were once disregarded as antiques has led to their promotion to the shelves and showrooms of the antique shops where they can be purchased—at a price. Certain aspects of nursery antiques, such as dolls, miniature furniture and early editions of picture books, have long been fashionable with collectors and are correspondingly expensive. But nowadays even clockwork toys have become highly prized and there is even a flourishing industry devoted to their renovation and repair.

As nursery antiques gradually creep up market it becomes increasingly difficult for the collector to embrace every aspect of the subject. This book presents a general survey of the field as a whole but the prospective collector would do well to consider a specific area or a single aspect on which to concentrate if any headway is to be made at all. Apart from the cost, limitations of space would probably force the collector to abandon indiscrimate and haphazard accumulation of unrelated objects. One would be wise, therefore, from the outset to concentrate on costume and accessories, or children's furniture, or games of skill and chance, or German pressed-metal toys, depending on the size of one's purse and storage space. As an alternative to this kind of single-subject specialization one could concentrate on a spectrum of nursery antiques relevant to a particular country in a specific period. Or perhaps a more thematic approach could be adopted, and the collection limited to games and toys of an educational character, or things which exploited the popularity of Shirley Temple and Mickey Mouse. The approaches to collecting are boundless, but one should always attempt to give some definite purpose to the objects collected, so that they possess collective as well as individual meaning.

1 The Nursery

The Victorian nursery was a world apart, generally a room or rooms on an upper floor, out of sight and sound of the rest of the house. Apart from romps in the garden or walks in the park, the average middle-class Victorian child might spend most of his or her life within its confines. The more palatial establishments might consist of several rooms: a day-nursery for playing in, a schoolroom for lessons, a night-nursery for sleeping in and separate rooms for the staff—head nurse, under-nurses, nursemaids and cleaners. At the other extreme one single large room might serve all these purposes, and the solitary nurse or nanny would have her own bed in one corner. Probably the average establishment consisted of a single nurse superintending her tiny charges in two rooms, the day- and night-nurseries.

Security was the watchword, hence the bars on the windows and the heavy and elaborate fireguard over the open hearth. The bars prevented toddlers from falling out of the window, but they must have represented something of a prison atmosphere. Many writers recalling their nursery days mention how they gnawed at the bars, like animals in a cage, in the hope of wearing them away. Apart from these security measures the nursery would have been a rather spartan establishment. Linoleum, waxed cloth or polished boards might be adorned by the occasional rug (the picture rug was a late nineteenth-century improvement), but carpets were rare. 'Hot shameful wee-wees on the nursery floor' (in the words of Jonathan Miller) would have been an all too common occurrence.

The furniture was seldom custom-built, at least not in its entirety. Oddments from other parts of the house, either worn or merely out of fashion, would be seconded to the nursery (in the same manner some quite passable antiques would be destined for the servants' quarters). A massive, bow-fronted chest of drawers might be situated, cheek by jowl, with a Georgian washstand and more modern beds of the brass rail and bedknob variety. Other items would be eternally fashionable in their functionalism and durability; the sturdy table and chairs of plain deal would have been similar to those used in the kitchen, bleached by innumerable scourings to remove spillages and stains.

A typical Victorian nursery;
Arlington Court, England

Folding screen decorated
with scraps and
chromolithographs; English,
mid-19th century

The draughts to which the upper storeys of most Victorian houses were prone were combatted by large folding screens, which stood in front of the nursery door and shielded the children. Early in the nineteenth century it became customary to decorate these screens with coloured pictures cut from periodicals, but by the 1850s numerous publishers in Germany, France and Britain were producing volumes of scraps—brightly coloured lithographs, which were die-stamped and required no skill to cut them out. Scraps and transfers were also used to decorate the smaller firescreens. In more recent times these ornaments were applied to the pastel-coloured surfaces of cots, desks and toy-boxes, but this would have been regarded as too frivolous in Victorian times. Children's furniture was usually stained or varnished in various shades of brown, unrelieved by any ornament.

Though the principal nursery table made no concession to the size of the children, other items were generally similar to adult furniture, but suitably scaled down. Unlike the robust tubular steel chairs and desks of the present day, these nineteenth-century pieces exhibited the same loving care and craftsmanship found in adult furniture. As already mentioned, judicious use was made of hand-me-downs from other parts of the house, but this does not imply that furniture specifically designed for children was not also produced. Chairs, stools and games tables (suitable for dolls' tea parties) were finely joined and turned in the prevailing styles. Desks were often fitted with tiny drawers and covered with embossed leather. They lacked the extravagances of marquetry and intricate mouldings and were usually more robust in construction; but otherwise these pieces were creditable examples of the joiner's and cabinet-maker's arts. What they may have lacked in elegant refinement they made up for in their miniature charm.

Certain pieces of furniture pertained to the nursery alone. The sleeping arrangements for the youngest children were surprisingly diverse, ranging from intricately woven Moses baskets and box-like contraptions known as arks, to sturdy cribs mounted on rockers and decorated with Jacobean-style carving. Larger children slept in cots, then, as now, fitted with high sides to prevent them falling out. The modern device of a drop-side seems to have come into use in the 1890s. Earlier cots had fixed sides, with wooden slats, turned wood or

Windsor cradle in maple and pine painted green; New England, *c.* 1800

13

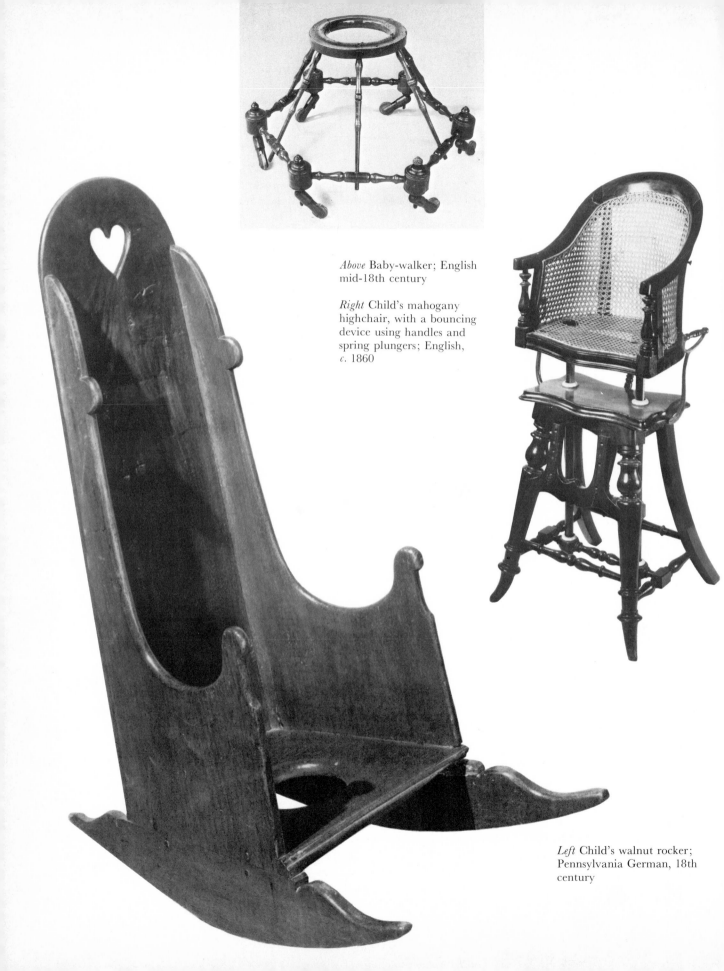

Above Baby-walker; English mid-18th century

Right Child's mahogany highchair, with a bouncing device using handles and spring plungers; English, *c.* 1860

Left Child's walnut rocker; Pennsylvania German, 18th century

brass rails and a surfeit of brass bedknobs in true Victorian fashion. Both cots and cradles may be found with sides constructed of wicker and rattan. Though children's furniture seldom reflected current taste in the way that adult furniture did, it should be noted that the bentwood craze (which originated in Austria) found its way into the nursery in the form of children's chairs, rockers and cribs.

Various devices for teaching infants to walk are used to this day. Baby-walkers have been in existence since the fourteenth century at least, since they have been recorded in woodcuts of that period. Two main types were produced: one resembling a low, four-wheeled cart with a tall broad handle, which the toddler could push along, and another consisting of a rectangular or circular frame mounted on wheels or castors, with the child inside. Many examples of the latter variety have survived from the seventeenth century, and are both elegant and complex in structure.

Infants' highchairs also became common from the seventeenth century onwards. The earliest type consisted of a tiny wooden armchair on very tall legs, and fitted with straps to prevent the baby from falling out. Later types were fitted with narrow ledges extending from arm to arm, serving the dual purpose of keeping the child in place and allowing it a small table for feeding. Considering the average size of a Victorian family, it is obvious that the highchair might well be in continual use over a period of twenty years or more, but the period during which any one child would require it would be fairly short. To make these chairs more useful, therefore, new styles were developed in the nineteenth century which enabled the chair to be adapted for other purposes. A popular form was the highchair which consisted of an ordinary small armchair mounted on a small table. The feet of the chair slotted into recesses on the table, and were held in place by wooden pegs; these could easily be removed to convert the highchair into two separate units. By the end of the century, however, more elaborate highchairs had been evolved so that the components could be dismantled to convert them into separate chairs, tables, baby-walkers or rudimentary go-carts. Highchairs played an important part in toilet training, it being a well-known fact that the bowels and bladder were more active while the child was feeding. Thus chairs were constructed with a circular hole in the seat and a chamberpot placed in a small shelf underneath, so that the small child could be 'potted' at meal times.

The lavatorial and ablutionary arrangements of the Victorian nursery were admirably self-contained. Although water closets and bathrooms with running water were becoming quite common as the nineteenth century drew to a close, the nursery continued with the practices of hygiene and sanitation which had long been universal. The wants of nature were relieved in the ubiquitous chamberpot. Curiously enough, although they probably enjoyed a later usage than full-sized adult chamberpots, the child's earthenware 'potty', with the same underglaze floral or Chinese blue-and-white ornament but having a smaller diameter and somewhat broader rim, is comparatively scarce. From

Group of four babies' plates; English and American, early 20th century

this it has been surmised that the majority of children's chamberpots were always more functional than the adult variety, and were usually made of enamelled iron sheet or painted tinware—neither being so comfortable or so conducive to good toilet training. To combat 'customer resistance', various patent potties were marketed with thick rubber rims (detachable and washable), but they were rapidly superseded by more serviceable bakelite pots at the beginning of the twentieth century, and these in turn gave way to the gaily coloured plastic potties, disguised as ducks or animals and decorated with pictures to distract the child's attention. The night-nursery might provide something more elaborate, in the form of a night-stool or close-stool, a cabinet containing a pottery bowl surmounted by a lidded lavatory seat.

Although most washstands were identical to those used by adults, some concession to the size of children was offered by special low cabinets whose lid lifted to reveal a wash-bowl. The inside of the lid was usually fitted with a looking-glass and sometimes brackets for toothbrushes and tumblers. When not in use the lid lay flat and the unit could be used as a table. A door underneath gave access to the slop-pail. Baby's bath was a daily ritual performed in front of the nursery fire. Even now, it is customary to bathe very small children in a special baby-bath, but in the days before indoor plumbing was common a bath before the fire was the usual practice for most children. A wide range of portable metal or even papier mâché baths existed, from the simple, chamfered rectangle which stood on the floor, to the elegant combined hip and nursery-baths which stood in a wooden frame supported by four legs. Baths were usually white-enamelled within and decorated with transfer-printed floral motifs on the outside.

Only babies were bathed daily; older children paraded on Friday evenings for a thorough scrubbing. Judging by the survival of numerous powders, lotions and unguents for the elimination of head or body lice, and the special combs and brushes required, the general standards of hygiene left much to be desired, though these problems had all but vanished from well-ordered households by the 1870s.

If the various autobiographical references to nursery life are to be believed, nursery meals were conspicuous by their frugality. Breakfast and tea were taken in the nursery itself, and only at lunchtime do the children of the middle and upper classes seem to have met their parents at the dining-table. By the 20s, however, the dichotomy of 'Upstairs Downstairs' had become significantly blurred to the extent that it was not uncommon for children—of the lower middle classes at any rate—to have lunch with the servants in the kitchen.

What the nursery diet lacked in variety was balanced to some extent by the scope of the crockery and cutlery used. Plates and dishes with motifs designed for children date from Greek and Roman times. Indeed, some Greek plates,

The Playroom at Sunnyside, N.Y., home of Washington Irving

which were obviously intended for children, carry motifs that are astonishingly erotic; the child was encouraged to eat up its food so that the picture could be studied. The same principle exists to this day, but modern children's plates and mugs have innocuous pictures—characters from fairy tales, folklore and television. Since the Victorians could seldom bear to see children indulging in pleasure *per se*, the pictorial motifs on crockery were often imbued with some didactic theme. The most common form consisted of the letters of the alphabet arranged around the rim. Others had texts or short verses of an 'improving' nature. All of the well-established potteries included children's crockery amongst their wares, so concentration on children's mugs and plates offers the collector a comparatively fresh angle on pottery and porcelain. More esoteric, perhaps, are the commemorative pieces—usually mugs—inscribed with the names of children and bearing dates of birth, christening, confirmation or coming of age. This charming custom, which was widespread in the eighteenth and nineteenth centuries, died out before the First World War. Bearing in mind the present interest shown by the public in commemorative wares in general, it is surprising that this practice has not been revived to any extent.

Children's cutlery does not afford the same scope as crockery, for the simple reason that there was always a wide variety of smaller knives, forks and spoons available without creating them specifically for children. Nevertheless, as spoons were the first implements that infants learned to handle, and it was an old-established tradition to give spoons as christening presents, there is a wide range in silver or electroplate, inscribed with the names of children and often bearing dates of birth. Spoons may also be found incorporating rattles or whistles in their handles, but relatively few had ends ornamented with tiny figures. Medieval silver or silver-gilt spoons decorated with the figures of Christ and His Apostles are now exceedingly rare. The custom declined in England after the Reformation, and so much silverware in general was melted down during the Civil War of 1642–9 that apostle spoons of the sixteenth and seventeenth centuries are virtually confined to museum collections. There have been various attempts in more recent times to revive the custom, but the more utilitarian christening spoon has been found preferable.

Special utensils were produced for the use of babies and infants. Today feeding-bottles are usually made of plastic, which is both lightweight and hygienic. Glass was widely used from the late nineteenth century until fairly recent years, and indeed it is still to be found occasionally. Glass bottles came in a wide variety of shapes—cylindrical, elliptical, rectangular, polygonal or banana-shaped—with or without gradations marked on their sides and frequently bearing the maker's name and trademark impressed along one side or on the base. Apart from the more functional shapes, however, feeding-bottles were produced in moulded or pressed glass of unusual shapes, such as

Babies' feeding-bottles, patent medicine, food warmer and rattles

Children's mugs; American, 19th century

animals, birds and fishes—no doubt in the hope of making the contents seem more appetizing. Many of the cylindrical or elliptical bottles had fairy-tale characters in relief on the sides, or occasionally were enamelled in different colours.

Earlier feeding-bottles were made of ceramic material, from tin-glazed earthenware and salt-glazed stoneware to fine porcelain and bone china. Only latterly do these bottles appear with the more whimsical decoration associated with nursery rhymes and fairy tales; the majority of examples have polychrome floral decoration or chinoiserie motifs in underglaze blue and white, which parallel the decoration found on adult crockery of the same period. Ceramic feeding-bottles were flask-shaped with a large aperture in the middle of one side and a neck tapering to a tiny lipped opening. The liquid was inserted through the aperture, which was then covered with the mother's thumb to control the rate of flow, while the baby sucked the liquid through the neck of the bottle. Glass feeding-bottles of the same shape may also be found, but by the middle of the nineteenth century the familiar rubber teat had been devised and bottles had wider necks over which the teat was placed. The wider neck enabled the bottle to be filled without recourse to a separate aperture in the middle, and this led to a simplification of the structure of these vessels.

When the baby was weaned, and moved on to solid or semi-solid foods, an aptly named utensil known as a pap-boat was employed. As babies take an inordinate amount of time over their food the problem of keeping the pap or gruel reasonably warm was solved by using special bowls or deep plates with a double bottom. Hot water was poured through a hole in the side of the rim and stoppered. The hot water circulated round the base and sides of the vessel and kept the food warm. Pap-boats and infant hot-plates may also be found decorated with nursery characters, and since variations of the latter have been manufactured to this day there are many different examples worth collecting.

After breakfast in the nursery came the morning walk, taken in all but the most inclement of weather. For the very youngest there was the baby carriage which, as its name suggests, was sometimes a miniaturized form of the open carriages then used by adults and drawn by horses. Baby carriages of this sort, with gleaming bodywork and elegant upholstery, were comparatively rare. Most conveyances were very functional in appearance, resembling small narrow tin baths on wheels. The earlier examples, fashionable for much of the nineteenth century and remaining in use well into the present century, were surprisingly deep, with the wheels attached directly to the bottom, and with a tall handle to allow the nurse to propel it without having to bend too much. With their inordinate love of long words derived from Latin or Greek, the Victorians dubbed these strange contraptions 'perambulators', but gradually the shorter form 'pram' became common. Towards the end of the nineteenth century more attractive styles began to appear. The body became lighter and higher, often made of wickerwork, thin wooden sheeting or painted tinware, and the inclusion of springs and the replacement of iron-shod wheels by rubber

Baby's feeding-bottle with
blue transfer-printed floral
decoration; Spode, early
19th century

Above Baby carriage from
the Tallman Toy Co.
Illustrated Catalogue, New
York, 1892

Perambulator; English,
1904

ones undoubtedly made for greater comfort. The earlier prams had a pushing handle behind the baby's head so that it lay or sat in the direction of travel. Later versions had the handle at the other end, so that the baby faced its nurse. Other refinements introduced towards the end of the century included sunshades, rain-hoods and rubberized pram covers. Successive twentieth-century developments consisted of braking devices, shopping panniers and, most recently, anti-cat nets.

A more advanced vehicle based on the original baby carriage appeared in the mid-nineteenth century and was the prototype of the modern pushchair. This accommodated older children and resembled a miniature landau, pushed from behind. The resemblance to adult carriages was heightened by the addition of a wooden horse fitted to the front, attached by cam-shafts to the wheels, so that it jogged up and down realistically as the carriage moved. On the borderline between toys (see Chapter 2) and baby carriages were various forms of animal—usually a dog or a horse—mounted on wheels and fitted with a pushing handle. Nineteenth-century examples were made of painted wood, though the saddlery might often be an authentically scaled-down version of the harness used by older children and adults. By the turn of the century, however, more realistic horses, with coats of real hide stuffed with horsehair or sawdust and equipped with realistic tails and manes, were coming into fashion.

Indoors, the child could expend some of its excess energy on a rocking-horse, sometimes referred to as a hobby-horse, although the latter was something quite different (see Chapter 2). Rocking-horses, consisting of a carved paint-ed figure of a galloping horse mounted on curved rockers, were in use by the second half of the seventeenth century, but did not become universally popular until the early nineteenth century. The more expensive models were made of real hide stuffed with sawdust, but the carved wooden horse painted dapple-grey was the most popular variety on both sides of the Atlantic. In the 1880s Dunkley's toyshop in London patented a new type of rocking-horse with an arrangement of bars and straps in place of simple rockers. This produced a most realistic back-and-forward movement, not unlike horse-riding, and it was considered much safer than the traditional rocker, since the heavy base ensured that it remained stationary. In more recent years all-metal horses (still painted dapple-grey) with jointed limbs have competed with the traditional rocker, but the latter is still a perennial favourite. Other features introduced in the early years of this century include the convertible rocker, with tubular steel rockers and retractable wheels. Dunkley's even produced a horse mounted on a tricycle undercarriage; the horse bobbed up and down alarmingly as the wheels turned.

For quieter moments the Victorian child had a wide range of diversions and pastimes. In an era before radio and television, children, like adults, made their own amusements. There was an abundance of games and puzzles, usually with an educational slant, and both boys and girls were expected to be skilled in the many minor arts and crafts of the period. They made their own

Tricycle and rocking-horse
combination; English,
c. 1870

amusements and allowed free rein to their fantasies in the games and charades
they devised. Such activities, however, were frowned upon when it came to
Sunday; outings to church and Sunday school were punctuated by such
decorous activities as needlework—perhaps a sampler with a religious text—or
reading an approved magazine, such as *Good Words*, or moral tales like
Bunyan's *Pilgrim's Progress*.

2 Toys

Toys, like the dolls discussed in the next chapter, are the oldest form of playthings. The simplest toys have been in existence for thousands of years, and many of them have remained basically the same down to the present day. Balls and marbles, hoops and tops may have become more gaily coloured or more sophisticated in composition, but they are the same today as children knew them and enjoyed them in Greek and Roman times. Other toys were not so universal perhaps, but were known in a particular locality for centuries before their introduction to the western world. The yoyo, the craze for which sweeps over Europe and America in every generation like some medieval plague, originated in China in the pre-Christian era, but did not make its début in Europe until the eighteenth century, being originally known as an émigrette. Various forms of diabolo and cup and ball have been found in such diverse regions as the Far East and South America and have subsequently become absorbed into the repertoire of European toys.

Although toymaking as an industry was well established in southern Germany in medieval times, and in France and England by the seventeenth century, the vast majority of toys until relatively recently were either the product of humble rural crafts, or things made at home by parents in their spare time, or even objects which children made for themselves. Even today a child's natural instinct seems to favour the simplest playthings and enormous satisfaction is derived from making even the most rudimentary toys for oneself. Although home-made toys possess great interest for the social historian and the ethnographer, they unfortunately lack the intrinsic value and aesthetic qualities that would commend them to the collector. The toys that are discussed here are those which would have been produced on a commercial scale, or possess evidence of craftsmanship and artistry in their composition. These are relative terms, and it must be admitted that many of the cheap, commercial toys of the nineteenth century were naïve in design and crude in manufacture, but none the less possess considerable period flavour.

Soft toys

Although soft toys are among the first playthings used by the youngest children, they are of fairly recent origin. Apart from rag dolls (see Chap-

25

ter 3) which date back to Roman times, soft toys in the guise of humanized animals seem to have been a late nineteenth-century invention. The earliest toys of this type consisted of nondescript ducks and amorphous sheep, but a major breakthrough came in the 1890s with the birth of the golliwog, based on the principal character in Florence Upton's Golliwogg (*sic*) stories, first published in 1895. This impish character with its black face, mop of hair and smart clothes was an instant success. In the stories he was always getting into mischief and in real life he served as a kind of scapegoat for many a child who could readily blame his or her own misdeeds on to 'Golly'. Racist overtones in more recent years have diminished the popularity of the golliwog, though it still ranks among the nursery favourites.

An altogether more innocuous creature, however, was the teddy bear, whose origins at the beginning of this century were nothing if not romantic. A political cartoon in *The Washington Evening Star* on 18 November 1902 alluded to the fact that President Theodore Roosevelt had baulked at shooting a tiny bear cub while on a hunting expedition in the Rockies. The bear cub in the cartoon inspired Morris Michtom, a toymaker, to produce a cuddly creature named Teddy's bear, and he went so far as to secure permission from Teddy Roosevelt to use this name. The presidential endorsement of course helped to sell the idea to the big toyshops and the teddy bear was an immediate success, laying the foundation of the fortunes of the giant Ideal Toy Corporation. The wheel has since come full circle, for the Ideal Toy Corporation was commissioned by the American government in 1962 to manufacture Smokey Bear, to publicize and popularize the work of the US Forest Service. There have been other offspring of the original teddy, including Yogi Bear and Rupert Bear (based on cartoon characters) and Winnie-the-Pooh soft toys, named after the teddy bear belonging to Christopher Robin Milne. Although the teddy bear originated in the United States, it rapidly spread to other parts of the world, taking on distinctive local characteristics. Thus European teddies, especially those manufactured in Germany, tend to be slimmer and longer-limbed, whereas British bears have the same chubby, stubby appearance as the originals. Other refinements which add variety to the teddy bear are bells concealed in the ears and various squeaking or growling devices concealed in the chest.

Other soft toys have come and gone, but the teddy soldiers on. The advent of Ming, the first giant panda at London Zoo in the 1930s, led to a rash of panda soft toys, and this cuddly looking creature with its oddly human features has since become a world favourite. As the symbol of the World Wildlife Fund its future popularity as a soft toy is assured. In the 1930s toy koalas began to appear in Australia and spread to America and Europe after the Second World War. These toys have the merit of being clothed in real fur (albeit kangaroo!). As the golliwog has slipped in the popularity ratings, its place has been taken by the troll, a grotesque creature of Scandinavian origin, and the gonk, a rotund individual with his eyes in his chest.

Bilboquet sticks; early 19th century

Wooden toys

The oldest and by far the largest category of toys consists of playthings made of wood. The universal availability of the raw material and the ease with which it can be carved into toys and dolls of all kinds are obvious factors. Numerous examples of wooden toys have survived from the Egyptian civilization of some 3,500 years ago. Carved and painted figures of cattle, horses and other animals, mounted on blocks with wheels attached, have been recorded from many parts of the eastern Mediterranean area dating back at least a thousand years before Christ, indicating that the principle of the pull-along toy was established at a very early date. Model carts and chariots with movable wheels were used as playthings in classical Greece. Conical wooden tops were in use in Egypt by 1400 BC and whipping tops in China by 1250 BC, if not earlier. The fancy tops used by children in south-east Asia to this day have probably remained the same for almost three thousand years. Similar tops from Africa and pre-Columbian America show how widespread a simple toy of this sort can be. Whipping tops were immensely popular in Europe and North America until this century, but have now been largely supplanted by tinplate humming tops operated by springs, plungers and other semi-mechanical devices.

The majority of wooden figures come under the heading of dolls and are more appropriate to the next chapter, but the range of carved wooden animals is enormous, encompassing almost every part of the globe. Many of these pieces are intricately carved and may be regarded as works of art rather than mere playthings. Often what began as a cottage craft, making toys for children, has developed in more recent times into a major souvenir industry. As a result these figures have become both more sophisticated and more stereotyped, lacking the naïve charm of the original toys. Carved crocodiles with movable jaws existed in Egypt three thousand years ago, and similar creatures are being carved to this day in the Middle East.

Left Carved and painted wooden top and grip; American, 19th century

Above Coach and horses in carved and painted wood with original box; German, early 19th century

27

Group of carved wooden
pip squeaks; American,
mid-19th century

Germany is the country most closely associated with wooden toys, largely on account of the fact that it was here that toymaking first became an important industry. Thousands of wood carvers were employed in southern Germany and Austria from the Middle Ages to supply an international market. Their wooden toys were intricately carved, cunningly devised and attractively painted; and though mechanization has overtaken this industry these wooden toys are still in a class of their own. The wooden toy industry was hard hit by competition from other countries, notably France, Britain and the United States, and by the use of various substitutes, such as plaster, papier mâché and latterly plastics; but the traditional woodcarvers managed to make a precarious living and their skills never died out. Since the Second World War the wooden toy industry in Germany has revived as the international demand for traditional toys has grown, and this has encouraged the development, or revival, of wooden toymaking in other countries, notably Russia and the Balkan states.

Although most of the carved figures were made in one piece, there were many examples of animals and humans with jointed limbs which could perform quite complicated manoeuvres by rotating handles or pulling strings. Acrobats and clowns, monkeys and dancing bears are among the most common, reflecting the eternal popularity of the circus. Animated wooden toys of this type were produced in Scandinavia and Italy, and from Pennsylvania to Japan, though the German figures are by far the most plentiful.

Inanimate objects made of wood also originated in Germany. Coaches and carriages, often with their attendant horses and coachmen, were being made in Germany from the sixteenth century at least and varied considerably in construction and detail. Those of Saxon origin were relatively crude, with solid blocks of wood forming the coach body and entire wheels carved from a single disc. The Bavarian coaches were generally of a higher quality, often with real leather upholstery, doors that opened and wheels in which the spokes were individually turned. The more elaborate examples even had tiny glass panes in the coach windows. By the 1840s robust locomotives, usually on the solid principle, were appearing in vast quantities. Like the toy boats and early cars and aircraft which were popular at the turn of the century up to the outbreak of the First World War, these wooden toys were usually basic in design, with scant regard to the real thing. Realistic models of different forms of transportation did exist, but these were always comparatively rare and belong more to the realms of model-making than to toys. The toy industry, as a rule, lagged behind the real thing by twenty years or more. Thus toy boats were still equipped with sails long after the advent of steam, and paddle-steamers were more common than twin-screw steamers. The construction of the early aircraft was so complex that toy manufacturers made no attempt to convey reality; early toy planes of the pull-along variety, with bird-like wings and clumsy fuselage, bore no resemblance to the Wright biplanes and Blériot monoplanes with which they were contemporary.

Another type of wooden toy was a more advanced version of the pull-along playthings that appealed to the younger children. Requiring more skill and co-ordination, and therefore suitable for older children, were push-along toys consisting of a large wheel or pair of wheels mounted on the end of a pole. The rotation of the wheels activated the arms and legs of a figure or animal. Ducks were a favourite subject, since the movement of the wheel could simulate the waddle of webbed feet admirably. Examples of this type of toy, with figures of birds, dogs, pigs and cows, date from the middle of the nineteenth century. A somewhat similar toy was the cock-horse. In its basic form this consisted of a pole surmounted by the carved head of a horse. The lower end of the pole

The master of ceremonies from a set of circus toys by Schoenhut; American, c. 1910

Wooden push-along horse; English, c. 1890-5

29

occasionally had a pair of small wheels side by side, but more often it was wheel-less and just trailed on the ground. More ambitious examples were equipped with rudimentary saddles attached to the pole about halfway down. The rider straddled the pole and jogged up and down in imitation of the real thing. Twin handles, projecting at right angles from the horse's temples, or a bridle and reins, enabled the rider to control his steed. More elaborate, and also of greater antiquity, were hobby-horses. These were elliptical hoops suspended from the body, with a wooden horse's head mounted at the front and a tail at the other. The framework was usually covered with fabric which simulated the rich caparisons worn by the heavy destriers of medieval knights. Hobby-horses of this type were popular in the sixteenth and seventeenth centuries but had virtually died out by the nineteenth century.

Tinplate and iron toys

To the mid-Victorians 'penny toys' meant cheap wooden toys, carved from a single piece of wood and brightly painted. They were sold by pedlars and street-corner traders, and were largely the product of small backstreet factories and sweatshops in Bristol and London. In the second half of the century, however, these cheap trifles were rapidly ousted by even cheaper toys stamped out of tinplate, crudely assembled and garishly painted. These tinplate toys originated in Germany in the 1860s, but were also produced in France and Spain on a very large scale. The majority of these penny toys were under three inches in height and were surprisingly lifelike in view of their mass-production methods. Many of them incorporated wheels, similarly die-stamped on the metal-button principle, and the rotation of the wheels triggered off a wide variety of actions. There were monkey knifegrinders, blacksmith gnomes, schoolmasters seated at their desks, shopkeepers and firemen, clowns and performing seals, nursemaids and prams, oarsmen and athletes, windmills and roundabouts, and even locomotives and early aircraft.

French and German tinplate toys were exported to Britain and the United States, although both of these countries eventually built up their own tinplate toy industries, and even reversed the trend by exporting their toys to the

Painted iron mechanical money-box; American, *c.* 1870

Cast-iron toy train;
American, mid-19th century

continent of Europe. In the United States the tinplate toy industry began in the 1840s as a sideline of tinplate manufacture, the old-established firm of Turners of Meriden, Connecticut, being the pioneer in this field. By the 1890s the tinplate factories of Philadelphia, New York, London and Birmingham were producing countless millions of these cheap toys. After the First World War similar trifles were mass-produced in Japan for export to other parts of Asia as well as Europe. Parents and teachers might rail against the dangers of lead poisoning from sucking the brightly coloured toys, or cutting oneself on the sharp edges, but penny toys continued to be immensely popular until the Second World War. Production ceased abruptly due to wartime exigencies and since then plastics have made them a thing of the past.

Cast-metal toys date from the early part of the nineteenth century (if we exclude model soldiers, which are dealt with in Chapter 5). Cast iron was used in Germany, the USA and Canada in the production of money-boxes and mechanical banks, an industry which expanded enormously in the 1870s and 1880s. The most familiar form was the Sambo; a coin placed in the negro's hand was swiftly transferred to his open mouth. Other banks featured hunters and bears, castles with movable drawbridges, cowboys and Indians and

Left Tinplate Lyons delivery van, complete with driver and sacks, and painted with advertisements and the Royal Warrant; English, *c.* 1910

Below Rare ice-cream tricycle by Taylor & Barratt; English, early 20th century

even corrupt politicians (the so-called Tammany Hall bank of the 1880s alluded to a notorious scandal in New York). More recent mechanical banks have been made in tinplate and seem to have been designed for maximum novelty appeal rather than security, since they are more easily rifled. In many instances quite intricate mechanism is triggered off by inserting a coin in the slot, so that figures of animals and people perform various actions. In others the insertion of a coin caused a clock pointer to rotate, thus registering the amount of money in the bank. Many commercial banks offered their customers metal money-boxes, and these often have the name and emblem of the bank cast or impressed on them.

Cast-metal models of motor cars, ships, locomotives and aircraft began to supersede tinplate versions at the turn of the century. The manufacturers of cast-metal models had one major advantage over their tinplate rivals—far greater accuracy. The demand for more realistic models probably dates from the First World War, when the general public became more keenly aware of mechanical things. Early manufacturers in this field were Dowst of Chicago and Tremo of Cardiff, noted for their fine miniature castings of cars and ships respectively. With the introduction of the Dinky series in the 1930s, however, British cast-metal models entered a new era, in which painstaking detail became all-important. Other companies, such as Triang, Timpo and Mettoy, and more recently Corgi and the famous Matchbox series, have challenged Dinky, but they remain pre-eminent in this highly competitive field.

Clockwork toys

Clockwork toys and automata originated as a sideline of the watchmaking industry in France, Germany and Switzerland and were highly developed by the middle of the eighteenth century. The majority of these early automata were made for the enjoyment of adults (who seem to have taken a rather childish pleasure out of such novelties), and the mechanism of these dancing figures and monkey orchestras would have been too delicate for the rough usage of children. These clockwork figures and groups were usually combined with simple musical boxes operating on the steel cylinder and comb principle. Wind-up toys of pressed metal developed in the second half of the nineteenth century and were confined mainly to relatively simple forms such as drummer boys, dancing bears, acrobats and tumbling clowns, roundabouts and carousels and other fairground attractions. Transportation was a limited field, confined to clockwork paddle-boats and comparatively crude and clumsy locomotives using a simple, circular track of large gauge.

In the age of steam, when every boy's ambition was to become an engine driver or railroad engineer, it was inevitable that train sets should have been immensely popular. The more affluent households could afford to give their children something approximate to the real thing—a working model of a steam locomotive, whose tiny boiler was fired by a spirit lamp. In the second half of

Jacks Golden Galloping
Horses: an electrically
driven model of a
fairground roundabout with
horses three abreast;
English, early 20th century

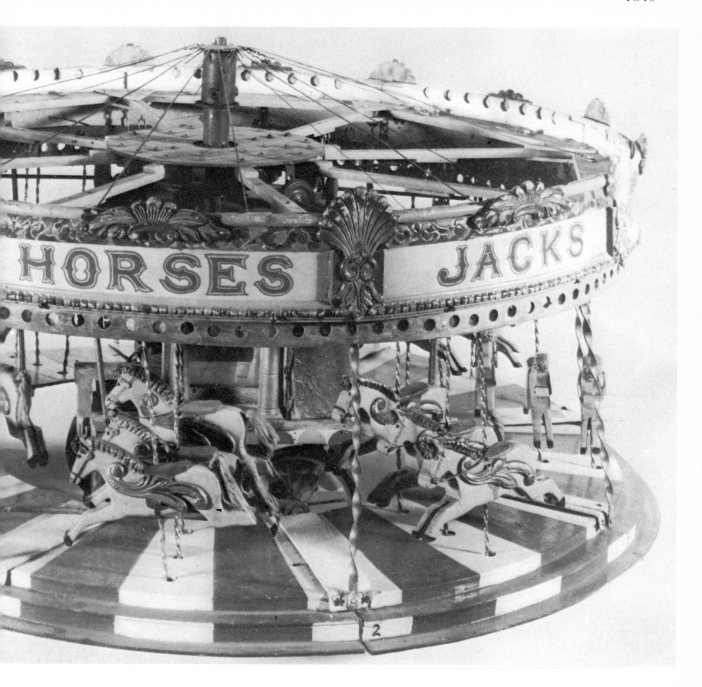

the nineteenth century Birmingham became the centre of an industry producing small locomotives which steered an erratic and leaky course across the nursery floor. These Birmingham 'steamers', as they were known, were quite functional in appearance, their iron or steel components painted black or dull green and relieved only by the gleaming brasswork of valves and pipes. The less well-off had to make do with a clockwork train set, but there was a vast improvement in their quality after 1900, largely as a result of the changes brought about by Frank Hornby, who pioneered the smaller 'double-0'

Above Clockwork and tinplate cat, clown and donkey, and mailman driving an ostrich, cast-iron pony and hansom cab; English, late 19th century

Right Model locomotive by Bing; German, *c.* 1890

Opposite Selection of penny toys; English, early 20th century

gauge, more realistic rolling-stock and equipment, and latterly replaced both steam and clockwork with electricity.

Electric-driven toys originated at the end of the nineteenth century, but remained a rarity until the 1920s. One of the early manufacturers in this field was Lines Brothers, who marketed a wooden truck in 1905 powered by a battery motor. Clockwork continued to be immensely popular, as the world became more mechanized, and vast quantities of tinplate cars, trucks, fire engines, road rollers, traction engines and military fighting vehicles rolled off the toy assembly lines in France, Germany, Britain, the USA and Canada in the interwar period. Since 1950, however, clockwork has lost ground in face of more compact battery or transistorized motors, and soon clockwork of any kind may become as much of an antique as steampower in the adult world.

Constructional toys

Educationalists and child psychologists have long known of the young child's keen desire to do things and make things for himself. Simple wooden blocks, segments and triangles in bright colours or in the natural polished state were widely used in Germany and the United States following the establishment of the kindergarten movement by Froebel in the 1830s, but alphabet bricks, with letters of the alphabet on one side and corresponding pictures on the other, were in existence even earlier. Both types have continued to flourish to this day. There was an immense upsurge of interest in building bricks for young children in the 1920s and 1930s, and a much wider range, including cylinders and cones, was made available to the public, who were now awake to the educational potential of such toys.

Building bricks for older children were fashionable in Germany during the second half of the nineteenth century. These *Steinbaukästen* were made of compressed clay, which resembled stone, and were decorated with transfer-printed pictures. They were usually smaller and in a wider range of shapes than the simple kindergarten bricks, but they suffered from the same limitations and it was very difficult to build anything complex that would not topple over at the slightest touch. The solution lay in devising some means of holding the bricks together. One solution was provided by Bako, which used bakelite bricks held together by thin metal rods. The rods were inserted into holes in a base-plate, like scaffolding, and the bricks slotted into place. Inevitably this system was not very flexible and was superseded by the principle of interlocking bricks. Minibrix pioneered their rubber bricks in the 1930s, the protuberances on one side locking into depressions on the reverse side of other bricks. This system was much more versatile, permitting a wide range of purlins, lintels and Corinthian pillars in addition to the more conventional bricks.

Nowadays both wood and rubber have been superseded by plastics in building bricks. The development of this aspect of the toy industry is vividly illustrated by the rise of Lego, which has truly been described as not so much a

Opposite Lucy, in a white muslin dress, with a fabric body and parian head, *c.* 1865; Marie, in a blue dress, with kid body and bisque head, French, *c.* 1875; pegwooden doll with fabric body and papier mâché head, *c.* 1845

37

Child's bricks decorated
with animals, numbers and
letters

toy, more a way of life. The original Christiansen factory in Billund, Denmark, manufactured wooden bricks of the conventional type, then progressed to plastic, non-locking bricks and later switched to the now familiar interlocking variety. The success of this business, one of the largest and fastest expanding of its kind in the world, lies in the versatility of its bricks, which appeal to the very youngest children and yet can be used by older children and even adults, from the simplest operations to the production of highly complex constructional and mechanical models (the latter assisted by special kits of motors and wheels). Whether Lego will ever be regarded as a 'nursery antique' is debatable; the durability and immutability of its standard components mean that, whatever new lines are added to the system, the basic range will remain unaltered for many years to come.

Constructional toys, such as Lego has now become, are historically more recent than simple building bricks. The first of the purely constructional toys was invented by Frank Hornby at the beginning of this century. Its original name of Mechanics Made Easy was changed to Meccano in 1907. In the intervening years Meccano has undergone many subtle transformations, so that although the basic principles of perforated metal parts held together by nuts and bolts remains the same, there is considerable variation between the early and later sets, and the former have now acquired a value far beyond their original retail price.

Constructional kits for model trains, cars, ships and aircraft are a major industry today, and although the present boom began during the Second World War (particularly for model aircraft), it has been in existence for almost a century. So-called Assembly Toys were produced in England from about 1870 onwards. The metal castings were very rough and the wooden shapes crudely cut, and it is difficult to imagine the Victorian youngster, with his passion for handicrafts of all kinds, being satisfied with them for long. At the turn of the century the situation improved dramatically. Bassett-Lowke, who originally manufactured fine working models of steam engines, subsequently diversified into scale models of ships, locomotives and aircraft. These kits were comparatively expensive, costing up to thirty shillings (£1·50–$2·70). They were extensively used by the armed forces for training purposes during the First World War, and expanded tremendously for sale to the general public in the 1920s. Model aircraft became all the rage in the 1920s as boys were fired by the exploits of the pioneer aviators. The toy manufacturers were not slow in exploiting this interest. Metalcraft of St Louis, for example, marketed a kit named appropriately 'The Spirit of St Louis', after Colonel Lindbergh's Ryan monoplane in which he made the first solo transalantic flight in 1927. The kit contained materials sufficient to construct twenty-five different 'airplanes that

Aeronautical toys of the 20th century: American constructional model of 'The Spirit of St Louis' with original box; Japanese models of Apollo X Moon Challenger, Satellite X-11 and Apollo Z; Lunar Bug, English

have made famous flights', according to the manufacturer's blurb. The kit retailed for less than a dollar and appealed to the lower, and less exacting, end of the market.

In recent years plastic has revolutionized the market in constructional toys. Cheap, accurate castings are easily handled and assembled, and in conjunction with modern quick-drying glues and paints enable the not-so-skilled to produce a thoroughly workmanlike job.

Cardboard or stout paper kits were marketed in Europe and America from about 1850. These sheets bore line diagrams of model omnibuses, locomotives, carriages, windmills, houses and famous public landmarks, and had to be cut out, folded, assembled and painted. More sophisticated kits were already painted and die-stamped so that they had only to be pressed out of their backing. These sheets came in packets or even in bound books with accompanying text and illustrations. On account of their relative cheapness card kits were revived during the Second World War for warships and military planes and vehicles, but although they still appear fitfully they have declined in face of the competition from plastic kits.

Educational toys

Apart from the alphabet bricks, whose twofold purpose is to teach the young child the alphabet and to encourage the development of constructional skills,

Ivory alphabet tiles and box; English, *c.* 1820

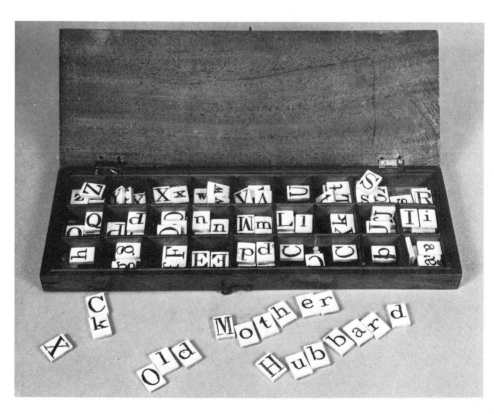

The Reversible Educational
Board; English, 1915

there are many toys with a didactic motive. Co-ordination of hand and eye was
fostered by various simple toys involving the insertion of cubes or cylinders of
different sizes into appropriate apertures in a base-board. A more
sophisticated form was the postbox developed in the United States with quite
intricate shapes to be inserted through corresponding slits in the lid of the box.
The earlier versions of the postbox were made of wood, but plastic is now used
instead. Other toys, such as the pile-driver, consisted of hammering pegs into
holes, or the stacking of beakers of ascending diameters within each other in
the correct order. The logical extension of the principle of fitting things into
their proper place is the board covered with assorted depressions corresponding to wooden silhouettes of simple objects familiar to young children: fruits
such as apples, pears and bananas, an ice-cream cone, a teddy bear, a top hat,
a ball and so on; or, for older children, an assortment of animals from the circus
or zoo. These boards originated in the late nineteenth century and were made
of wood covered with brightly lithographed pictures. More modern examples
were usually made of some stout card composition substance and are not so
easy to find in fine condition, since the silhouettes are easily damaged by
attempts to force them into the wrong space.

Quite a number of instructional toys are concerned with arithmetic. The
abacus, widely used in medieval Europe and in Asia to this day for
accountancy purposes, has long been recognized as an important method of
teaching children the rudiments of counting. Variations on the counting
frames of beads strung on rods are shallow trays with sliding counters in
polished wood, ivory or plastic materials. The more advanced forms of
educational toys, requiring greater intellectual exercise, are discussed with
games and puzzles in Chapter 4.

3 Dolls

Dolls are among the oldest of human possessions, being found in both primitive and sophisticated societies and in every form of civilization from the Neolithic to the present day. Many dolls, especially those of the greatest antiquity and those associated with ethnography, were never intended as children's playthings and are thus beyond the scope of this book. But although it is obvious that a terracotta or bronze figurine of some ancient deity had religious rather than juvenile significance, the borderline between the mystical and the childish is often obscure. This is particularly true of dolls emanating from Japan and the Indian tribes of America. Children's dolls belonging to the latter are found in many parts of the American continent, varying in composition and dress from one tribal area to the next. These dolls were often modelled on the images of deities and were entrusted to the child as part of its religious instruction. They were to be treasured carefully rather than played with. Even to this day the elaborate dolls of the Pueblos are regarded as taboo and their sale is forbidden. The children's dolls of the Keres Indians are extremely stylized and resemble the prayer sticks used in religious ritual.

The vast majority of extant European dolls dating from Greek and Roman times are undoubtedly in the religious category. Certainly the more durable forms of cast bronze and baked clay range from identifiable idols to fertility symbols. Children's dolls are understandably rarer because they were carved from wood or made from stuffed rags. Sufficient examples have survived, however, to prove that children two thousand years ago enjoyed the same basic playthings as their descendants do today. In medieval Europe many dolls had a religious significance connected with the images of saints and often associated with Christian festivals such as Easter and Christmas. The best example of this is the Nativity scene, erected in churches and private houses to this day, in which the Christ child was displayed in its crib with more or less elaborately costumed figures of the Holy Family, the Shepherds and the Magi in attendance. Curiously enough many of these early figure compositions were enshrined in a baby's cradle, transformed for the occasion into the room at the inn or an outdoor scene, complete with miniature furniture, utensils, crockery and implements. Eventually special cabinets were produced for this purpose, but the old names of *crèche*, *krippe* and *nacimiento* (used in France, Germany and Spain respectively) were retained. In the

Opposite English wax doll, *c.* 1850-75, dressed in a set of clothes *c.* 1820-5

43

Protestant countries of northern Europe, especially in the Netherlands, Scandinavia and England, the crèche was replaced by a more formal structure out of which developed the doll's house or baby-house, discussed in Chapter 5.

While more or less primitive dolls existed everywhere as children's playthings it was in southern Germany, and especially in Nuremberg, that doll-making as a highly organized industry first emerged. As long ago as the middle of the fifteenth century doll-makers were grouped into guilds, each devoted to the production of specific types of doll or accessories. An equally elaborate system of middle-men and distributors ensured that pedlars and street traders in every part of Europe were stocked with Nuremberg dolls and toys, and as a result these late medieval German figures are to be found in museums from Scotland to Turkey. Many of these early figures had some religious significance. Even when they cannot be identified as a particular saint, they often have pious expressions or poses which point to some devotional significance.

Prior to the late seventeenth century the more elaborate and expensive dolls would have been produced for a specific purpose. While it is true that the daughters of the upper classes had expensive fashion dolls as playthings, the majority of the dolls in this category were produced for utilitarian purposes. Dolls exquisitely clad in the latest styles were produced as a sideline of the French fashion houses in the seventeenth and eighteenth centuries and were intended for export to other European countries, and latterly to America, where they were in great demand from *couturières* and milliners. These fashion dolls were known as mannikins, and the French term *mannequin* has survived to this day to denote a fashion model.

At the other extreme the children of the lowest classes had to be content with home-made rag dolls, but in between the two extremes came the dolls of the middle classes. These dolls had finely carved heads, coated with gesso and painted with lifelike features. Their bodies were made of pieces of turned wood, pinned or strung together to simulate joints. Greater mobility and realism was effected by attaching the arms and legs to the torso by means of cloth hinges or leather straps. The finish of torso and limbs was often poor compared with the face and hands, indicating that these dolls were primarily intended as the peg on which clothes were meant to be hung.

The jointed wooden doll was manufactured all over Europe, but was most closely associated with England, and probably continued to be made in that country long after it had declined in popularity elsewhere. French and German dolls were being made with bisque clay heads from the seventeenth century onwards, and the gradual relaxation of import duties on these dolls in the eighteenth century led to an increase in their popularity in Britain. The early pottery dolls were capable of a more realistic expression, but were comparatively fragile and inevitably suffered grievously in the hands of careless owners. Eighteenth-century Continental dolls were provided with fine porcelain heads, but these were comparatively rare. The head and bust were

cast in one piece, and holes were drilled in the base of the bust so that it could be sewn on to a cloth body. During the nineteenth century porcelain dolls became increasingly popular, and many of the smaller porcelain factories in southern Germany regarded them as their main stock in trade.

At the same time there was a revival in the painted wooden doll, hand-carved in great quantities in Austria and northern Italy. Some attempt to inject realism into these dolls was made by fitting them with wigs of real hair, or by fitting the heads on to stuffed leather bodies. But the great majority of these 'peg-wooden' dolls were of an all-wood construction with hair indicated by paint. These mass-produced wooden dolls were widely known as Dutch dolls—a corruption of *Deutsch* (German)—and were particularly popular in the late nineteenth century, their robust constitution making them a nursery favourite of younger children. Nevertheless the bullet-headed sameness of these dolls impelled manufacturers to look for ways and means of ousting their rivals with more interesting and attractive dolls, without increasing the cost of production.

In endeavouring to find a substance that would rival porcelain the European doll manufacturers hit upon various composition or wood substitutes, of which papier mâché became the most popular. Plaster of Paris, paper pulp and glue were combined to make a substance, both light and durable, which could be moulded to form hollow heads. The doll's head could then be finished with a coating of wax to simulate flesh and painted to give a life-like expression. Plaster of Paris and chalkware dolls were also produced in the nineteenth century, but were more liable to chipping and cracking. They were much heavier than papier mâché and, since they had to be cast solid, were more costly in materials.

45

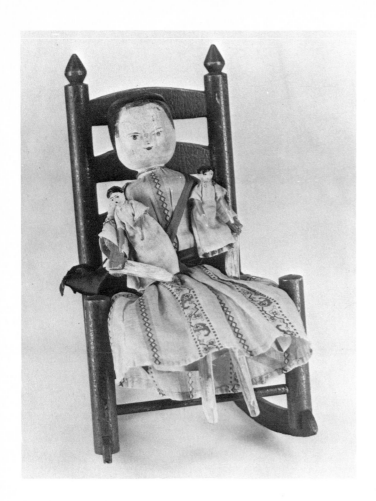

Above Pegwooden doll with twin babies in a rocker; Pennsylvania German, 19th century

Right Jointed wooden doll with painted facial features and hair; English, 1832

Papier mâché dolls' heads were a speciality of several manufacturers in the town of Sonneberg in Thuringia, including Cuno and Otto Dressel and Adolf Fleischmann, though it should be noted that many other types of doll, both carved wooden and porcelain, were also manufactured there. Papier mâché heads were prepared from pulp forced into sulphide moulds taken from an original clay model. The inclusion of glass eyes and some attempt to add hair imparted an air of realism to these dolls, which the more traditional wooden dolls generally lacked. Moreover, papier mâché was a substance that easily lent itself to mechanical processes, and by the middle of the nineteenth century the vast majority of the cheaper dolls were produced in this substance. At first only the heads were made of papier mâché, the torso and limbs being of stuffed leather or cloth, but eventually even the bodies were cast in papier mâché. The composition of this substance varied enormously, and several patents were taken out in Europe for similar materials which more closely imitated human flesh in texture. Towards the end of the nineteenth century subtle improvements were made in the surfacing of papier mâché heads, and many of the baby dolls of the early 1900s have remarkably realistic features. Papier mâché and similar composition substances continued to be used for cheap dolls until the advent of plastics revolutionized the industry after the Second World War.

Porcelain dolls

If papier mâché catered to the cheaper end of the doll market, porcelain was reserved for the most expensive dolls. It would seem to be a simple step from the exquisitely modelled statuettes of Meissen, Nymphenburg and Frankenthal to similar work in the form of dolls, but there is little evidence to show that porcelain was used for this purpose much before the early years of the nineteenth century. Isolated examples of porcelain dolls have been recorded in Germany which have tentatively been ascribed to the period 1750–80 on account of the styling of the hair and other features, and some dolls' heads and limbs of fine porcelain have been discovered bearing the marks of the Nymphenburg and Berlin porcelain factories of that period. Nevertheless, porcelain was such a very costly material at that time that its application to dolls would have been impractical. The rare exceptions would have been dolls made for ladies, rather than the playthings of little girls, and thus they are not relevant to this book. Significantly, these very early porcelain dolls represent adults and are dressed accordingly. By the 1820s however, porcelain dolls began to appear with the chubby features of babies and young children and these were obviously designed as the playthings of the daughters of the wealthier classes.

Very few of the German porcelain dolls of the nineteenth century bear makers' marks, but each potter seems to have had his own characteristic style of denoting hair, painting the eyes or making provision for sewing the head to the body. In the majority of cases the hair is moulded as an integral part of the head and merely indicated by painting; but in a few instances discs or patches were incorporated in the crown on to which a doll's wig might be fixed. The bodies of these dolls were of stuffed leather or cloth, or occasionally of jointed wood. The earlier dolls had the hard glaze associated with German porcelain of that period, but by the mid-nineteenth century matt-surfaced bisque porcelain was being employed, since it gave a more realistic impression. Many of the late nineteenth-century dolls are known as parian heads, from the hard porcellanous material known as parian ware resembling marble. This material was widely used by the French and German manufacturers, though the English manufacturers (who had first applied parian ware to statuary) do not seem to have used it for dolls.

The German monopoly of porcelain dolls was dented in 1843 when the Parisian potter Jacob Petit began producing doll's heads, though the fact that his mark is seldom found would seem to indicate that doll production was, at best, a sideline to his main activities. As the century wore on the German potters managed to cut their costs and mechanize their processes so that they flooded the world's toy markets. Conta and Boehme of Possneck are, perhaps,

German doll with porcelain head and limbs, and European heads, mid-19th century

47

Porcelain doll in a wicker
carriage with sunshade;
American, *c.* 1905

the best known of these cheap porcelain manufacturers, mainly because of the
china fairings and other porcelain trifles which they supplied to the world
souvenir market, but their dolls are competently modelled and were
deservedly popular in the period up to the First World War. They produced a
wide range of dolls, including some which were entirely made of porcelain and
cast in one piece. These small porcelain baby dolls were known as *badekinder*
(bathing children) since they could be immersed in water without detriment.
They were even provided with dolls' bathtubs. Very tiny porcelain dolls were
also produced by the Thuringian manufacturers to inhabit dolls' houses.

   Up to the time of the Franco-Prussian War the French doll-makers imported
porcelain heads from Germany, adding their own bodies and having the
elegant clothes hand-sewn by hundreds of out-workers who laboured in

48

Bisque doll by Jumeau;
French, *c.* 1890

the sweatshops of the Paris backstreets to earn a few *sous* a day. After the ephemeral experiments of Petit in the 1840s Ferdinand Gauthier seems to have produced bisque porcelain dolls' heads in the 1860s in competition with the German imports, but it was not until after the disastrous war of 1870–1 that the French made serious efforts to produce dolls' heads for their own requirements. The Parisian firm of Jumeau, established about 1840, built a new factory at Montreuil in 1873 and included a pottery in which porcelain heads and limbs were produced. The factory was arranged on the most up-to-date lines and covered every aspect of doll production. Jumeau continued to manufacture the elegantly dressed dolls which were the lineal descendants of the fashion dolls, but their name is best remembered for the famous Jumeau *bébés* – modelled as babies or young children with wide-eyed expressions and

49

Swivel-headed bisque doll
by Bru, *c.* 1880

Character doll by Kammer
& Reinhardt, *c.* 1910

plump features. These dolls were fitted with porcelain heads, hands and feet, jointed limbs and bodies of a composition substance. Great care was taken with the manufacture of the glass eyes, which gave to Jumeau dolls a most realistic appearance. Real hair was modelled with painstaking care to reproduce the coiffures of the period.

The Jumeau dolls were in a class of their own and the company was jealous of the fact. The dolls were clearly impressed with the firm's trademark and the boxes in which they were sold bore lengthy advertisements for the factory and enumerated the medals and diplomas awarded in world's fairs from Philadelphia to Melbourne. Other manufacturers appeared in the latter part of the nineteenth century and of these Bru came closest to rivalling Jumeau in output and quality. Others whose dolls are now highly prized included Pintel, Rabery and the German firm of Fleischmann and Blodel, which had a Parisian branch under the name of Eden Bébé. These lesser companies, however, were squeezed out by their German rivals, who undercut them in the medium- and low-priced market, and by Jumeau, which dominated the more expensive range. Eventually these lesser companies were absorbed by Jumeau, which formed the combine known as Société Française de la Fabrication des Bébés et Jouets (usually known by its initials SFBJ) and continued to produce fine porcelain dolls up to the outbreak of the Second World War.

Many of the French porcelain dolls of the late nineteenth century had the recognizable features of contemporary celebrities, such as Queen Victoria and Jenny Lind, and this type of historic doll was also widely manufactured in Germany, with the addition of the whole galaxy of German royal ladies, from the Kaiserin Augusta Viktoria downwards. Towards the end of the century, however, the better-class German manufacturers challenged the supremacy of Jumeau by producing their own version of the *bébé*. Cuno and Dressel of Sonneberg, already noted for their papier mâché dolls, were one of the first companies to evolve a more child-like head than heretofore, but by 1890 the Waltershausen companies–Kammer & Reinhardt, Handwerck and Kestner–and the Koppelsdorf firms of Heubach and Armand Marseille, were also engaged in the manufacture of German dolls with *bébé* heads. Foremost, however, was the company of Simon & Halbig, of Ohrdruf in Thuringia, who not only produced dolls' heads for their own use but supplied them to other doll-makers.

Simon & Halbig in particular were keenly aware of the vast export market, and produced an enormous variety of good quality dolls catering to specific areas and interests. They were probably the first company to produce Oriental and Negro dolls, originally aimed at the American market but later widely popular elsewhere. Armand Marseille produced dolls which were frankly aimed at the Parisian market and, with their coquettish expressions, were no mean rival to the fashion dolls or *poupées modèles* of an earlier generation. Heubach specialized in dolls with different expressions. Previously dolls had a rather vapid expression on their faces, but now Heubach provided his

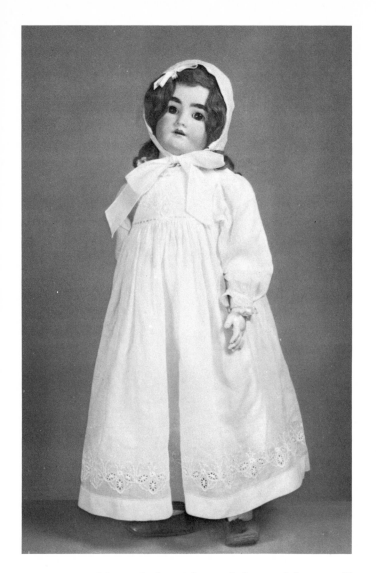

customers with a choice, of puzzled, tearful or smiling countenances. By contrast, many of the German porcelain dolls at the turn of the century had rather grotesque expressions and disproportionately large heads. The trend towards 'character' dolls continued in the early years of this century and the much more realistic features of Kammer & Reinhardt's 'Baby' doll of 1910 gave rise to the canard that it was modelled on Crown Prince Wilhelm or even Kaiser Wilhelm II himself as a baby! Soon Kammer & Reinhardt were producing a whole family of character dolls, each given a distinctive boy's or girl's name. These German dolls were usually sold with the barest minimum of clothing and it was left to the purchaser (or his wife and daughters) to sew the clothes to his own taste. French dolls, on the other hand, were generally provided with a complete trousseau.

The German inroads into the French market were checked by the First World War. At the same time the English potteries, which had had very little

Left Bébé cosmopolite, with bisque swivel head and composition body, ball joints and sleeping eyes, in French lawn dress, by Simon & Halbig, *c.* 1900

Above Bisque doll by Armand Marseille; German, *c.* 1900

to do with the manufacture of dolls' heads, were encouraged to produce them. The firms better known for their Goss china ornaments–Goss of Stoke-on-Trent and Ridgway of Shelton–were the first in the field, but several others, notably Mayer & Sherratt of Longton and the Blue John factory of Hanley, continued to manufacture porcelain dolls' heads up to the time of the Second World War. After 1918, however, the Germans rapidly recovered their pre-war markets, and as a result English porcelain dolls are relatively scarce. Eventually celluloid, and later modern plastics, sounded the death-knell of porcelain and papier mâché dolls alike.

Wax dolls

Wax has been used since the earliest times as a modelling material, and waxworks have been recorded from the Middle Ages onwards. Small wax effigies of the Holy Family, the Magi and the Shepherds also featured in many of the medieval Christmas cribs, and thus it was an easy transition from the religious dolls to playthings of a more secular nature. The techniques of wax modelling developed enormously in the second half of the eighteenth century, giving rise to wax portrait plaques and such waxwork tableaux as staged by Marie Tussaud in London. Wax dolls, with heads cast in a plaster mould, are thought to have been made in Germany from about 1760 onwards. The hair was modelled in the wax and glass eyes were set into wax sockets to give a more realistic appearance. These early German wax dolls usually had snub noses, hence the term *Stulpnäse* by which they are often known. The original poured-wax technique was not only costly in materials, but the resulting dolls were rather fragile and noses and ears could easily be rubbed off or distorted. A more effective method was to produce papier mâché heads, subsequently coated with several layers of wax to give the impression of real flesh. Alternatively, wax heads could be built up in successive layers stiffened by fine muslin.

The biggest problem facing the makers of wax dolls was the hair. As the vogue for real hair was established in porcelain and papier mâché dolls of the nineteenth century, the wax doll-makers tried to compete by fixing hanks of hair to the crown. At first this was done rather crudely by inserting the end of the hair into an incision in the top of the head. These dolls were popularly known as slit-heads, but unfortunately the slits tended to widen into longitudinal cracks which eventually split the doll's head in two. Moulded simulated hair might be satisfactory for cheap wax dolls, known as 'squash-heads', but the more expensive types required real hair. The problem was finally solved by two doll-makers of French extraction resident in England, Augusta Montanari and her son Richard Napoleon. The distinctive feature of the Montanari dolls was the way in which each strand of hair and each eyelash was painstakingly inserted into the wax by means of a hot needle. Not surprisingly, Montanari dolls were exceedingly expensive and as their output was never high, relatively few of these costly dolls have survived.

Wax doll; English, 1807

Doll with wax head, bust
and limbs, and cloth body
modelled by Montanari on
Princess Louise; English,
c. 1853

The Pierotti family, of Italian extraction but engaged in the manufacture of
waxworks in London from about 1780, also entered the doll market and
continued to produce fine wax dolls until shortly before the Second World War.

Charles Marsh was one of the few indigenous English doll-makers working
in this medium and he produced dolls with wax over papier mâché. His dolls,
with their blue eyes and flaxen hair, had a distinctly 'English' look about them,
whereas the Pierotti dolls have aptly been described as 'Italianate'. Charles
and John Edwards produced many excellent wax dolls in the 1870s. Very rare,
but not particularly attractive, wax dolls were also made by Herbert Meech,
Doll Maker to the Royal Family. Wax dolls had a fairly brief life, being
eclipsed by the new German and French bisque-headed dolls at the turn of the
century. Nevertheless Henry Pierotti continued to make luxury dolls in this
idiom until shortly before his death in 1935.

Rag dolls

One of the oldest and cheapest types of doll is the rag doll, homely yet cuddly and probably inspiring more affection in the long run than her more elegant wax or porcelain cousins. The rag doll has been recorded from Greek and Roman times, and in different guises has been found all over the world down to the present day. Most early examples, however, have disintegrated and even the better preserved rag dolls of the nineteenth and early twentieth centuries all too often show signs of having been loved not wisely but too well. From the collector's viewpoint there are several types of rag doll which are of considerable interest. Curiously enough it was the Montanari family, famous for their high quality wax dolls, that gave the rag doll a more elevated status. Richard Montanari produced a cheaper version of his wax dolls, consisting of cloth bodies stuffed with sawdust. The head was an integral part of the body in true rag-doll fashion, but its face consisted of a thin wax mask stiffened with muslin. Most of the surviving examples of these Montanari rag dolls, dating from the early 1880s, show signs of wear, facial cracks or amorphous patches where the wax has melted in the hot grasp of their youthful owners.

The vast majority of rag dolls were home-made from any old scraps of available material. This is not to decry the rag doll, which often possesses great sociological and ethnographical interest on account of the wide variety of materials used, not to mention the skill shown by the seamstresses in the finish and clothing of these dolls. Rag dolls in the true sense were first marketed

Printed cotton sheet for making a Christmas doll; American, late 19th century

commercially in 1908, when Henry Samuel Dean, whose famous rag books had been launched five years previously, extended the idea to 'toy sheets' – pieces of calico, on which were printed the outline of a doll's body and face, with the patterns for the various items of clothing on a separate sheet. Many of the early Dean rag dolls were sold ready made-up, and in the period up to the First World War there were many improvements, such as the 'Tru-to-Life' face, 'Tru-Shu' feet and various styles of wig. Dean rag dolls have continued to appear down to the present day, though many of them cling to the traditional designs evolved in the early years of this century.

Raggedy Ann doll, based on the character created by Johnny Gruelle

Not surprisingly, this was a field in which the German doll-makers also excelled, and the finest collectors' pieces emanated from Germany. The most highly prized dolls are those rather grotesque cloth dolls produced by Margarete Steiff, characterized by a button in the ear (her trademark) and a hideous squint. Steiff dolls were much criticized in France (one may detect some chauvinism here) on account of the squint which was said to be encouraging French children to imitate it! By contrast, Käthe Kruse aimed at realism rather than surrealism in her rag dolls. Her sculptor husband undoubtedly assisted her in the sensitive modelling of the dolls' features. Käthe Kruse did for the cloth doll what Kammer & Reinhardt did for the porcelain doll, breaking away from the vacuity which characterized dolls' features prior to that time. Kruse dolls were beautifully hand-sewn in towelling material and were comparatively expensive – which rather defeated the object of the exercise. They continued to be made from the early 1900s until after the Second World War. Since then they have been translated into an entirely new medium – plastic.

Rubber and plastic dolls

The doll-makers of the nineteenth century continually strove to find satisfactory materials which would result in cheaper and more durable dolls without sacrificing the qualities of realism and charm of the finest porcelain and wax dolls. The traditional papier mâché dolls of Thuringia underwent various transformations, as noted already. It was a Thuringian emigrant living in Philadelphia who took papier mâché a stage further and foreshadowed the plastics of the present day. Ludwig Greiner took out a patent in 1856 for an improved composition which included scraps of fine cloth, such as silk and muslin, to give the material greater strength. The end products were marketed as 'Greiner Everlasting Doll Heads'. The Greiner patent was renewed in 1872 and dolls of this type continued to appear down to the end of the nineteenth century. The fact that so many of them have survived to this day demonstrates the truth of Greiner's description.

Rubber dolls are of surprising antiquity, Goodyear having given a franchise in 1850 to Benjamin Lee of New York, who manufactured dolls in indiarubber. Unfortunately rubber is the most capricious of substances – attractively supple when new, but becoming brittle and perishing with age. The very few mid-nineteenth-century dolls now preserved all exhibit distortion of limbs and deep cracks, their original paintwork having flaked off long ago. Rubber dolls have continued to be popular ever since, but as potential collectors' items they are best avoided. Hollow-moulded rubber dolls date from the end of the nineteenth century, and became an instant success as a bath-time toy, to be floated and bathed at the same time as their owners. Those with built-in squeaking devices date from the early years of this century.

Celluloid, a synthetic substance whose principal ingredients were cotton, camphor, alcohol, with nitric and sulphuric acid, was developed in the late 1850s and applied to the manufacture of cheap dolls from the late 1870s. Celluloid was more durable than rubber, but it proved to be a dangerous material whose inflammability was no doubt the cause of many nursery fires. Celluloid dolls originated in the United States, but by the end of the century they were also widely manufactured in western Europe, and spread to China and Japan in the 1920s. Despite frequent condemnation on safety grounds, celluloid dolls continued to proliferate and did not decline in popularity until the advent of new and safer plastic substances in the 1950s.

Novelty dolls

Apart from a relatively small number of dolls which sought to portray actual persons, few European dolls of the nineteenth century could be considered as novelties or gimmicks, pandering to some current craze. The reverse was true in the USA and Canada, where novelty dolls were rapidly developed in the second half of the century. The disadvantage of most European dolls was that, no matter how realistically their features were modelled, the dolls themselves remained immobile. In the United States the Co-operative Manufacturing Company patented a type of doll in 1873 with articulated limbs made of wood with metal hands and feet. These dolls, known as Patent Mannikins, were capable of an infinite variety of postures, adding greatly to their realism. Subsequently other American manufacturers developed spring or elastic-jointed dolls and ingenious devices which permitted the doll's head to be rotated and moved up and down quite freely.

From the jointed doll of the 1870s the next step was the walking doll. Automata and clockwork dolls were developed in Germany and Switzerland as a spin-off from the watch- and clock-making industry of the seventeenth and eighteenth centuries, but as they were designed primarily for adult delectation they are outside the scope of this book. Self-moving, non-winding dolls, however, were evolved in the 1880s, incorporating intricate systems of weights and balances and using spring-loaded joints to create a naturalistic effect. Ingenious clockwork mechanisms applied to walking dolls were, in fact, rather earlier, the best-known being the *Autoperipatetikos* (a jaw-breaking Greek word meaning 'self-walking') patented by Enoch Morrison of New York in 1862.

Mechanical walking doll;
German, *c.* 1860

The stiff, gliding movement of the Autoperipatetikos was limited by the
relatively crude limb-jointing of that period. By the 1890s, however, the
combination of clockwork mechanism and limb articulation enabled the
American manufacturers to market large-sized boy and girl dolls which not
only walked but moved their heads and arms in a realistic manner. European
walking dolls of the second half of the nineteenth century relied heavily on their
clockwork mechanism for propulsion and cheated by having the doll
supported on wheels (concealed beneath long dresses), or relied on such
contrivances as a perambulator or wheelbarrow which the doll ostensibly
pushed along in front.

The talking doll has a surprisingly long history, the earliest examples having
been produced in the 1820s by Johannes Mälzel of Regensburg. These figures,
which are regarded as automata rather than dolls for children to play with,

57

Bisque doll with moving
eyes; French, *c.* 1890

contained a clockwork mechanism which activated valves producing 'pa-pa'
and 'ma-ma' sounds. It was not until the invention of the phonograph by
Edison in the 1870s, however, that a talking doll in the true sense was possible.
The Edison Talking Doll made its début in 1890, and consisted of a doll which
concealed a tiny phonograph inside her chest. These dolls were fitted with
robust steel bodies, though their bisque heads and jointed limbs conformed to
the prevailing fashion. Interchangeable records of nursery rhymes and songs
gave the talking dolls a wide repertoire. It was not long before the Edison dolls
were being copied in Europe, Jumeau of Paris being prominent in this field.
The *Bébé Phonographe* appeared in 1895, and soon talking dolls of a similar type
were being produced in Britain, Germany and other European countries.

58

At the same time, numerous improvements had been made in the mobility and features of dolls. Here again Jumeau seems to have been the principal innovator, producing the sleeping doll with movable eyelids in 1885–6. The rival firm of Bru produced the *bébé teteur*, which took liquid from a baby's feeding-bottle in a most realistic manner. Inevitably this was followed by dolls whose diapers required to be changed, indicating the extent to which realism could be taken in late Victorian times. Bru also patented a breathing doll whose asthmatic condition was hardly likely to endear it to its youthful owners. The turn of the century was the heyday of the mechanical novelty doll, and the manufacturers on both sides of the Atlantic vied with each other in producing expensive dolls whose accomplishments were seemingly infinite. The First World War and the subsequent Depression killed the market for such costly novelties, and manufacturers turned instead to the production of cheap dolls for the mass market.

Character dolls

Mention has already been made of the golliwog and the teddy bear which originated in the period 1895–1903, but the turn of the century also witnessed the birth of several character dolls, mainly in Canada and the USA. In 1888 Palmer Cox published *The Brownies: Their Book* and exploited the enormous success of these gnome-like characters four years later by marketing a series of rag dolls known as the Palmer Cox Brownies. Oddly enough, Beatrix Potter herself hoped to transform Benjamin Bunny and her other characters into dolls but the idea was never developed (though porcelain figures of the Beatrix Potter characters have been very popular in more recent years).

More ephemeral sources inspired dolls as well. Rose O'Neill's cartoons for children in *Ladies Home Journal* (1909) formed the basis for the Kewpies, quaint little creatures with bulging eyes and a distinctive top-knot. The adventures of the Kewpies (a name derived from 'cupids') led to booklets known as Kewpie Kutouts and these, in turn, led to the first Kewpie dolls, patented in 1912 and originally made by Kestner of Germany for export to the United States. The earliest Kewpies were made of bisque porcelain, but they were later manufactured in a wide variety of materials, from cloth and rubber to celluloid, chalkware and wood, and since the Second World War have been up-dated in various plastics. Eventually Kewpie dolls were copied all over the world, though they never enjoyed a wide measure of popularity in Britain. Their place in the United Kingdom was taken by a similar range of character dolls, produced by Chad Valley in the 1920s and based on the well-known postcard characters drawn by Mabel Lucie Attwell. Where Rose O'Neill's Kewpies had a certain gauche charm the Attwell children combined well-scrubbed plumpness with knowing looks that reflected the sophistication of the postcards. Significantly, although Mabel Lucie Attwell postcards and cartoons have endured to this day, the dolls did not survive the Second World War; the

Right American Kewpie dolls, *c.* 1920 by Rose O'Neill and *c.* 1940, and matching doll's china teaset *c.* 1910

Below Composition jointed baby dolls, each in flannel baby wrap and pink trimmed blanket, nestling in a basket—a contemporary souvenir of the birth of the world's first quintuplets, Emile, Yvonne, Cecilie, Marie and Annette, to Mrs Olivia Dionne at Corbeil, Ontario, Canada, on 28 May 1934

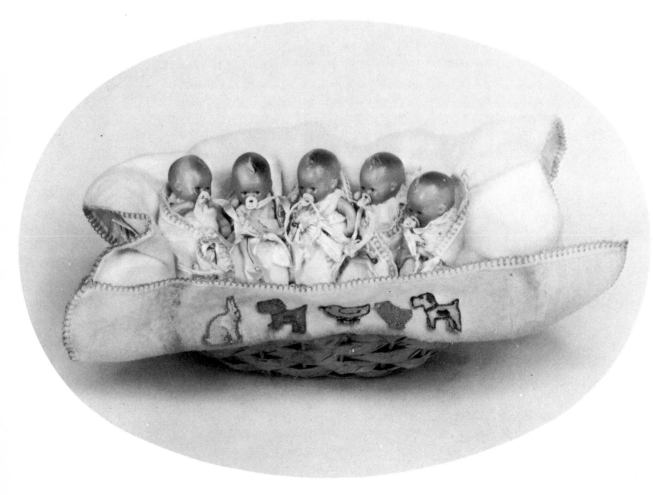

cartoons have an enduring appeal for adults whereas the cherubic but worldly-wise dolls did not have the same appeal to children.

Character dolls based on real-life children were relatively unknown in the antique period and were confined to a few half-hearted attempts at featuring the Prince of Wales and other children of Queen Victoria. Nearer the present day, however, the heyday of motion pictures between the world wars gave rise to a number of child stars whose names were associated with a wide range of products and who lent their features to character dolls. Jackie Coogan, who rocketed to stardom by up-staging Charlie Chaplin in *The Kid,* was among the first of the child actors to be reproduced in dolls wearing the large floppy cap which was his trademark. The Ideal Toy Corporation estimated that they sold over 1,500,000 dolls in the 30s modelled on Shirley Temple. Dolls modelled on the British princesses, Elizabeth and Margaret Rose, were never a commercial proposition, but sets of dolls based on the Canadian Dionne quintuplets were marketed in North America shortly before the Second World War.

Miscellaneous dolls

The fascination for miniature items (see Chapter 5) no doubt inspired the pedlar doll, which seems to have been a British phenomenon dating from the early nineteenth century. These dolls were often made in pairs, representing an old man and his wife, and dressed in the clothing worn by the pedlars who took their baskets of assorted wares from village to village. The chief interest of these dolls lies not in their own construction (which was often comparatively crude and home-made) but in the wealth of trinkets and tiny bric-à-brac with which they were equipped. The earliest dolls were made of any available material, with carved wooden heads, rudimentary bodies and clothing sewn from odd scraps. In some cases dried fruits or potatoes were used as heads, cured by various processes to produce a leathery surface which could then be painted. Tiny articles of clothing or household implements – the pedlar's stock-in-trade – were made by hand and either sewn or glued directly on to the pedlar's clothing, or arranged in a wide, shallow basket. The more elaborate (and probably later) dolls had large trays laden with miniature boxes, crockery, trifles and trinkets, and the most intricate of all were equipped with entire market stalls. The pedlar dolls of the latter half of the nineteenth century consisted of bought German or French dolls, suitably dressed and equipped, and the fun lay in seeking out miniature novelties to add to the pedlar's stock. The revival of interest in pedlar dolls in more recent years has led to a certain number of 'reproduction' dolls of this type, complete with assorted knick-knacks. Although pedlar dolls were used as children's playthings, they undoubtedly appealed to adults as well and provided the perfect vehicle for a collection of miniature objects.

A large group of dolls consists of puppets and marionettes, used as a form of entertainment for thousands of years and recorded in every part of the world,

Paper doll and a selection
of costumes based on the
ballet dancer Marie
Taglioni; American, 1835

from ancient Greece to modern Indonesia. Many types of puppet belong to
the world of ethnography rather than nursery antiques, while the elaborate
shadow puppets of south-east Asia possess ceremonial and religious
importance. Cardboard figures, with limbs jointed by metal rivets and
agitated by means of thin cords, became popular as children's toys in the
eighteenth century and have continued to this day in many different guises. In
France these marionettes were known as *pantins*, after the village of Pantin,
where they are thought to have originated. They were the ancestors of two types

of doll – the dancing doll, marionette or puppet on a string, and the cardboard cut-out doll, provided with cut-out sheets printed with clothing and dress accessories. Cardboard or paper dolls became popular in the 1870s and were either static (provided with a slotted stand) or mobile (articulated with pins and strings), the former being the type used in the pastime of doll-dressing. The origins of glove puppets are shrouded in the mists of antiquity, but they were well established in medieval Europe and continue to this day in the perennial favourite, Punch and Judy, as well as in many European variants and local equivalents. Glove puppets, with papier mâché heads and gaily coloured bodies, became popular nursery toys in the nineteenth century and continued through the period when 'do-it-yourself' home entertainment was at its height. The majority of extant examples were undoubtedly home-made and modelled on the characters of the traditional Punch and Judy theatre. A development of the glove puppet modelled on the character of Mr Punch was the Punch-in-the-Box, with a stuffed leather head and long cloth body concealing a powerful spring, which was released when the box was opened. By the nineteenth century such devices were known by their present name of Jack-in-the-Box. Few of the puppets and marionettes of the antique period were commercially manufactured; only since the postwar advent of television, which has given a new lease of life to the art of puppetry, have dolls in the form of humanized animals (from Muffin the Mule to Sooty and Basil Brush) become popular with children on a large scale.

Jack-in-the-Box clown with papier mâché head; American, mid-19th century

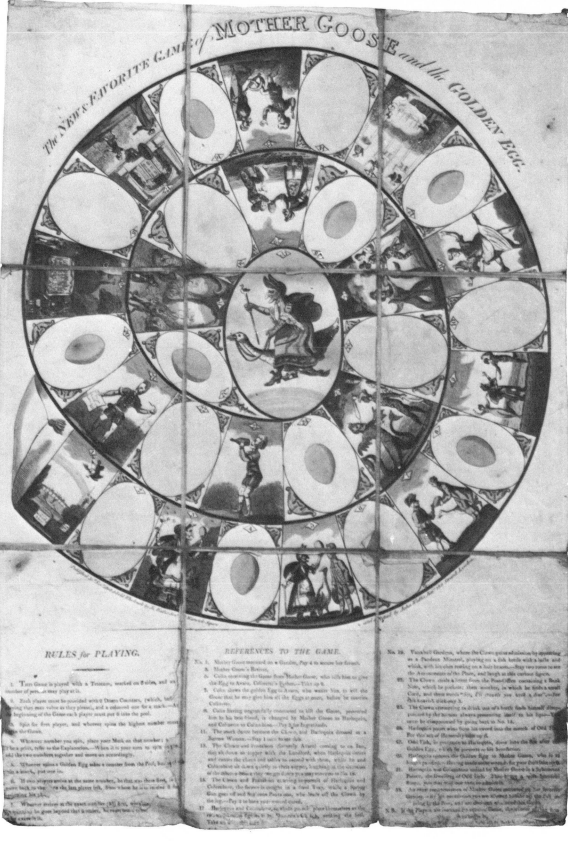

The NEW & FAVORITE GAME of MOTHER GOOSE and the GOLDEN EGG.

4 Games and Puzzles

Many of the more basic games played by children have been recorded, in some form or other, in Greek and Roman times. Many examples could be cited of friezes and pottery depicting children playing with balls, tops, hoops and knucklebones. Medieval woodcuts, illuminated manuscripts and a few paintings indicate that such games were not unknown in the fourteenth and fifteenth centuries, though actual examples of the equipment associated with these games seem to be very rare. Either they were too ephemeral for preservation or children had less time for play than later generations. Many writers have commented on the fact that there was a significant increase in the attention paid to children's games from the beginning of the eighteenth century onwards. The Puritan attitude towards games and frivolity of any kind is understandable and would certainly explain the dearth of games material in seventeenth-century Britain; but similar views on children's leisure activities seem to have been held in other parts of Europe at the same time.

Handling games

Games which combined an element of chance with skill in using one's fingers or the co-ordination of hand and eye were immensely popular two thousand years ago. The prime favourite was knucklebones, known to the Greeks and other Mediterranean peoples and relying solely on a basic material which required no alteration and was readily available. Actual bones were widely used in medieval times, but the game seems to have declined in popularity thereafter, until it was revived in the eighteenth century. By the late nineteenth century it was at the height of its popularity, and imitation knucklebones were made of carved hardwood, ivory or even cast metal. Pressed wood and other composition substances were used in the manufacture of knucklebones, often painted in different colours. In the present century the game of knucklebones has declined again though it survives fitfully to this day.

Small glass balls resembling marbles have been recovered from burial sites in the Mediterranean area dating back some three thousand years, but their purpose is not known. It is probable that they had some religious significance and highly unlikely that they were associated with a form of game. Significantly, though Egyptian, Greek and Roman frescoes and friezes depict

Opposite The game of Mother Goose and the Golden Egg, played with a teetotum; English, 1808

65

Set of seven felt animal skittles, the five bowls in the form of rabbits and a kangaroo; English, *c.* 1900

knucklebones and dice-throwing, marbles are not represented at all. Nevertheless solid glass balls as children's playthings were in existence by the fourteenth century, being among the objects produced by the glass bead makers of Venice. These marbles were prepared from a solid glass rod, often containing strands of different colours. Small sections were broken off, mixed with sand and charcoal, and put into an iron receptacle, which was rotated in a furnace to produce completely globular pieces. After cooling, the marbles were shaken together in a bag to remove grit, sand and charcoal, and finally polished. Venetian marbles were produced in opaque glass of different colours as well as transparent coloured glass. Coloured or opaque strands created a *latticinio* effect, and the inclusion of air bubbles increased the variety. Venetian swirls, ranging in size from half an inch to two inches in diameter, spread to other parts of western Europe by the eighteenth century and were always the most highly prized of all marbles.

Glass marbles were widely imitated in France, Germany, the Low Countries and England and reached their peak in the second half of the nineteenth century, but there were many other kinds of marbles. Dutch stonies were balls made of Coburg stone in Germany. Chinamen were large pottery marbles fired in a kiln with a distinctive glaze of black-and-white bands. Plain pottery marbles were known as taws or alleys taws. A blood alley was one streaked with red pigment. Bouncers or toollies were enormous marbles, the size of cricket balls, produced in the Sunderland district about 1850. Glassies, pure and simple, were the small plain marbles used at one time to seal mineral water bottles. These ingenious bottles are comparatively scarce nowadays since the vast majority of them would have been broken to extract the marbles. At the beginning of this century steelies were a popular substitute for glass marbles and consisted of hollow steel balls imported from the United States. Although marbles in some form or other had been played since the end of the Middle Ages, the game in its present form was a nineteenth-century invention and reached epidemic proportions about 1870. Like many other children's games it has since languished, though it is interesting to note that it has witnessed a revival in recent years as a serious adult pursuit.

Set of spillikins in wood and ivory; Russian, *c.* 1840

Jigsaws

Dissected puzzles, as jigsaws were originally known, originated in England in the second half of the eighteenth century and the earliest examples were almost invariably maps. They consisted of printed and hand-coloured sheets, which were more of a compendium of information than the pictures they later became. In appearance they resembled the packs of educational playing cards which were also popular at that time and were undoubtedly produced with the same intention – to impart useful knowledge to the young in the painless guise of a game. Just as the arrangement of the playing cards in proper sequence

Historical and geographical dissected puzzle by Peacock Brothers of London, *c.* 1914

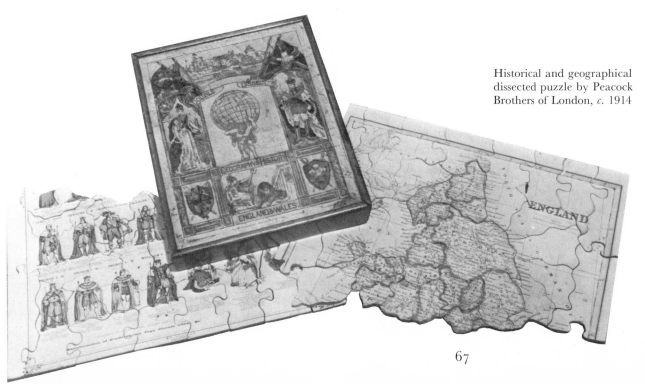

produced a connected narrative, the arrangement of the pieces to form a composite whole enabled the player to build up the story or lesson. The early examples have more text than picture and often consist of small vignettes which make up a larger picture when assembled. This technique was particularly suited to the teaching of history (with processions of kings and queens) or geography (with tiny pictorial motifs and matching text set against the background of a map). The pieces were simply cut, the lines dividing them being only slightly irregular so that the wrong pieces would not match up. At that time a blade capable of making intricate patterns had not been evolved.

Early nineteenth-century puzzles became more pictorial and less verbose, and by about 1840 they were beginning to take on their present character. The cuts were more irregular and the principle of interlocking was beginning to develop, but the pieces were still comparatively large. Although the imparting of knowledge was still paramount, by the 1860s there was an increasing number of pictorial puzzles that depicted fairy tales, biblical scenes and current events. The invention of the jigsaw in the 1870s led to the development of intricate fretwork as a decorative feature of furniture, but it was not long before this technique was being applied to dissected puzzles. Pieces became

Right Locomotive puzzle by Milton Bradley of Springfield, Mass., 1868

Opposite Late 18th-century American jointed wooden doll, which belonged to Little Miss Proctor, who is shown holding her in the portrait above by Charles Willson Peale

much smaller and shapes infinitely varied. At the same time the didactic element gradually died out and purely pictorial puzzles emerged. Many of these pictorial puzzles must have presented a problem to their users since the lid of the box seldom reproduced the picture itself; this practice did not become commonplace until the end of the century. Chromolithography was being used as a printing process by the 1890s and continued into the twentieth century. Both photogravure and letterpress were used increasingly from the 1920s to reproduce colour photographs of portraits and scenery. At the turn of the century lithograhic reproductions of famous paintings were fashionable, but there were still many jigsaws featuring biblical scenes or historic motifs. The old name, dissected puzzles, lingered on until after the First World War. Few of the nineteenth-century jigsaw puzzles exist today with all pieces intact; those that do would now command a high premium.

Opposite Group of toys, mid-late 19th century: a cup and ball, building bricks, three tops and a teetotum, and glass marbles, including two bouncers

Playing cards

Like the early dissected puzzles, playing cards were aimed at the diffusion of knowledge in a palatable form. Instructional cards have a very long history, dating back to the early seventeenth century in England, France, Italy and Germany. The packs, often irregular in number, were based on existing packs of tarot and other playing cards, and imparted information on a thematic basis, grouping related objects, such as castles and cathedrals of Europe, kings and queens, historic landmarks, the counties of England and Wales, birds, animals, scientific discoveries and heraldry. The didactic element spilled over into the playing cards which were used by adults, and many sets of the

Below Didactic card game featuring the Welsh counties, dated 1818

seventeenth and eighteenth centuries, while marked with the familiar hearts, clubs, diamonds and spades, also carry pictures and text on their face. Playing cards of this type, often with vignettes of a political nature, survived to the end of the nineteenth century. A popular form was the pack of cards which posed questions and gave the answers on alternate cards, the text being matched by appropriate pictures. When arranged in sequence the story would unfold in a logical manner. This type of 'question and answer' card game, though rather stuffy by present-day standards, was highly popular in the late nineteenth century.

Children's card games of the early nineteenth century were usually deadly serious. The Welcome Intruder, a game dating from 1815, was an interrogatory card game in this vein and it must have been rather boring after a time. Inevitably there was some reaction against the appalling didacticism of these playing cards, and this is evident in the curious examples of home-made playing cards of the early nineteenth century. Both children and adults drew their own designs on plain pasteboard cards and evolved their own light-hearted (and sometimes *risqué*) card games.

The reaction against the serious playing cards was first exploited commercially in the United States. Anne W. Abbott of Beverly, Massachusetts invented a jolly card game for the amusement of her own family and based it on a comic character called Dr Busby. She sold the idea to the printers and publishers Currier and Ives, and the first commercial version of Dr Busby appeared in 1843. Though now long forgotten, it was a great success at the time on both sides of the Atlantic, and paved the way for later games which remain favourites to this day. Prominent among these is Happy Families, devised by a Mr Jacques in 1861. It originated in Britain but has since spanned the globe and now appears in many different, localized versions. Animal Grab, dating from about 1890, was a much rowdier card game which reflected the greater relaxation in children's amusements by the turn of the century. Many other playing card games appeared in the period from 1890 to 1920, often of great ingenuity and intricacy but whose novelty soon faded. Today these are among the card games now most highly prized by collectors.

Board games

Playing cards arranged in the traditional pack of four suits were also used in conjunction with many of the board games developed in the second half of the nineteenth century. Games such as Pope Joan required a combination of cards, counters or discs, and a special board – in this case a circular tray divided into eight compartments labelled Ace, King, Queen, Knave, Game, Pope, Matrimony and Intrigue. Other board games incorporated an element of chance, which was determined by the throw of dice. The old Puritanical revulsion against dice as tools of the Devil died hard and such objects were forbidden in many Victorian households – at least so far as the children were

Dr Busby card game by Parker Brothers; American, 1914

concerned. The taboo on dice was evaded in various ways. One was to use special children's dice which were uniface, with dots marked on one side only. Of course, this involved the use of six or eight dice, which theoretically could yield either a high score or no score at all. It seems to have been a typically Victorian piece of humbug to use such pieces, when traditional dice would have been much neater.

The other method of indicating a score, much favoured in Victorian times, was the teetotum, a small disc divided into coloured and numbered segments, which was rotated like a top. When it came to rest the number on the segment resting on the table gave the score. A more elaborate device was the repulsion bell, which operated on similar principles to the roulette wheel. The age-old antipathy towards dice gradually vanished as the century wore on, and by the 1870s gaily coloured dice-cups were becoming quite acceptable.

Board games which depended on the element of chance, popular since the Game of the Goose was developed in the eighteenth century, consequently developed enormously in the latter part of the nineteenth century. There were many games relying on the throw of the dice or the spin of the teetotum for the number of moves made by the players across a marked board. The basic principle of these games was the same, but variety was imparted in the pattern of the board, the markings on it and the objects used to denote each player's position. Thus the Game of the Race consisted of a racecourse with a number of fences, ditches and other obstacles at certain intervals, and the players used

73

tiny figures of racehorses. The earlier examples had horses of cast lead, but by the turn of the century stout card figures on a small wooden base were more common. Other games in the same genre had a more didactic slant. A good example was The Travellers, in which moves were made across a map with landmarks and other places of interest indicated in the numbered squares. A popular basis for this game was the map of England or the map of Europe. Variations of this took the form of an itinerary, with the route from London to Edinburgh, for example, winding snake-like over the board showing the towns and their mileages in the numbered squares. A considerable amount of accurate detail was incorporated in the boards of these mid-nineteenth-century geographical games. Neglected by map-collectors, they are highly prized by students of Victorian parlour games.

Many popular games of the late nineteenth and early twentieth centuries had their origins in the Orient. This applies particularly to games in which the player's skill, rather than the element of chance, was important. Chess, an adult game of Indian and Persian origin, is the finest example of this type, but is outside the scope of this book. There were other games of Oriental origin, however, which had a great appeal to children and adults alike. The oldest of these was called Fox and Geese and came from India to western Europe in the late seventeenth century. Pieces were moved across the board at right angles or diagonally, the aim being for the 'fox' to capture the 'geese'. Similar principles were involved in draughts or checkers, using disc-shaped pieces, or in Chinese checkers in which small marbles moved across a board with specially constructed depressions. Draughts and checkers have remained perennial favourites to this day, but though the basic design of pieces and boards is unaltered there is considerable variety in the style and construction, while the boxes in which the games were packed usually have a quaint period flavour in their pictorial designs. The early game of Fox and Geese gave way to a similar board game known as Asalto. An interesting version, popular in Britain in the 1860s, was known as Officers and Sepoys – an allusion to the Indian Mutiny of 1857. This variation used a board on which a small area in a different colour represented the beleaguered fort, held by the officers against the mutinous sepoys.

The Indian inspiration of this version was highly topical, but other games emanating from that part of the world were of much greater antiquity. The Mogul rulers of India in the late sixteenth century had an elaborate game played on a checkerboard courtyard with slave girls as pawns and the moves of the emperor and his courtiers dictated by the throw of cowrie shells. This life-sized game was known as Pachisi and its configuration inspired the board game of Ludo, introduced to Britain from India towards the end of the nineteenth century. Somewhat earlier, the game of Halma relied on a checkerboard with perforations in each square so that the pieces could be slotted into place. Each player had nineteen 'men' grouped in camps at opposing ends of the board, and the object was to move the men across the board and occupy the enemy's

Home-made checkerboard; New England, early 19th century

74

The Grocery Store game by
Parker Brothers; American,
1889

camp. Undoubtedly the most complicated game of Oriental origin was Mah
Jong, introduced to the West from China in the late nineteenth century. Apart
from chess, this game was probably the most decorative of all board games, and
often much skill was lavished on the carving and ornament of the boards, pieces
and special dice used.

Towards the end of the century more elaborate games began to appear, with
boards which were more specifically linked to some aspect of life. From France
came L'Attaque (the Attack), a more advanced and sophisticated game
derived from Asalto and foreshadowing the war-games and *Kriegspiel* discussed
in Chapter 5. A preoccupation with the grim reality of the First World War
probably led to the decline of this once popular game, but attempts have been
made to revive it in recent years. Far more enduring, however, was Monopoly,
launched in the 1930s and still going strong. It was descended from a mid-
Victorian board game called Moneta, which combined elements from the
world of banking, property and commerce. The basic structure of Monopoly
has remained unchanged over the years, although the styling of the boards,
pieces and the special cards and imitation money has varied from time to time.

Moneta and Monopoly may have been designed to inculcate sound business
principles in the minds of the young, but other games were aimed at improving
their word-power. The Victorians were particularly fond of word games and
spelling bees, and this explains the popularity of Logos, the ancestor of
Scrabble.

From the foregoing one would tend to form the impression that even in the

The Game of Anagrams,
published by Pease &
Warren, New York, 1875-95

matter of nursery games the Victorian child took things very seriously. There
were some board games, however, which provided little or no intellectual
stimulus. Chief among these was bagatelle, the forerunner of the modern pin-
table, and tiddlywinks whose apparent inanity (to the uninitiated) is often
regarded as the ultimate in useless activities.

Puzzles

Magic squares and blocks, interlocking cubes and similar puzzles of
arrangement are of great antiquity and examples have been recorded in China
dating back well over a thousand years before Christ. They operate on the

76

principle of locking pieces of wood, pottery or metal, of different sizes and shapes in a set sequence, so that the components are dovetailed into a complex structure. The puzzle lies in putting the pieces together, and conversely, dismantling them again. Of comparable antiquity, and also emanating from the Far East, are puzzles consisting of twisted metal rods or wires, seemingly locked together for all time, but easily taken apart once the secret technique is mastered. These Chinese puzzles were not widely known in western Europe until the latter half of the nineteenth century, when they were popularized commercially and continue to fascinate and irritate children to this day.

Naturally, it was not long before European and American toymakers began producing their own variations on these ancient themes. Popular puzzles dating around the turn of the century included the Persian Shah puzzle and the Egyptian mummy puzzle (the latter no doubt inspired by the fashion for Egyptology that culminated in Lord Carnarvon's discovery of Tutankhamun's tomb in 1922). Valentine of Dundee struck a patriotic note with their Allied Flags puzzle launched during the First World War, and there were many others of an ephemeral nature, but the traditional Chinese puzzles continued to be the paramount favourites.

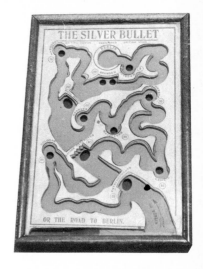

The Silver Bullet, a British 'patriotic' game of First World War vintage

In the 1890s a new type of puzzle was evolved which, under numerous guises, remains popular to this day. This type consisted of a small glazed box containing several small silver balls. The problem was to get the balls all lying in the little depressions provided in the base of the box. By careful tilting and shaking of the box one could often manage to get two out of the three into their niches, but on trying for the third the other two would be dislodged and the whole maddening process would begin all over again. The variety in such puzzles lay in the decoration of the base-board – comic portraits, scenery, landmarks, fairy-tale characters and nursery-rhyme incidents being the most common.

Dating from the early years of this century are pocket-sized puzzles consisting of sliding pieces which move up and down or across in relation to each other. Eight, and occasionally fifteen, pieces are arranged in the form of a square, with one blank space to permit movement. Pieces engraved with letters of the alphabet are the commonest, and are used as a word puzzle, but other versions have numerals or the symbols from packs of playing cards inscribed. These variants require the player to arrange the pieces in arithmetical or geometric progression, or in ascending numerical order, or in sequences associated with card games, as the case might be. The early examples were made of metal with polished wood pieces, but later artificial substances, such as bakelite, perspex and other forms of plastic, have been used instead.

5 The World in Miniature

Much of the charm in many nursery antiques lies in the fact that they are very small–miniature replicas of objects associated with the adult world. The heyday of the nursery miniature was the second half of the nineteenth century, when it was possible to acquire almost anything in miniaturized form, and a large industry in Germany and other European countries was geared to this production. Tiny examples of pottery, glassware, furniture, metalwork and other articles were manufactured for a variety of reasons. Many of these miniatures were produced as trade samples, and replicas of everyday objects, especially those made in silver, were produced as elegant toys and trinkets for the delectation of adults rather than children. Special cabinets, designed to display silver 'toys' and miniature glass and porcelain, were a feature of many drawing rooms in France from the middle of the seventeenth century, and this delightful custom soon spread to Italy, Spain, Germany, the Low Countries and eventually to Britain. Silver models of animals, human figures (especially of Chinamen, reflecting the craze for chinoiserie) and tiny wagons, windmills and other semi-mechanical contraptions were the fashionable playthings of adults up to the end of the eighteenth century. Frivolity of this sort went into decline about the time of the French Revolution and never recovered. In subsequent generations many of these miniature objects of vertu were handed over to the children of the wealthier classes and inevitably suffered as a result. They were never intended as children's playthings and nowadays they have recovered much of their former status as collectors' pieces. Strictly speaking, therefore, they should not be regarded as nursery antiques although the borderline between miniature *bibelots* and children's miniatures is often shadowy. Mention has already been made of the tiny objects connected with pedlar dolls, and it is certain that the bulk of the juvenile miniatures were produced for a specific purpose, as part of the furnishings of dolls' houses or the equipment of toy shops.

Dolls' houses

The modern doll's house is a familiar object which, in Victorian and Edwardian times, was the pride and joy of many a nursery. It evolved out of the

Opposite The doll's house that belonged to Beatrix Potter at Hill Top, Sawrey

79

Left Miniature bed in
mahogany (11 in high);
New England, *c.* 1790-1825

Above Room for a doll's house with a fine array of glassware, crockery, cutlery and hollow ware; English, 18th century

Left Miniature writing table in oak veneered with walnut (5 in high); English, late 18th century. This may have been an apprentice piece, but such items often found their way into the nursery and were used in dolls' houses.

Nativity cribs of the Middle Ages and the elegant display cabinets noted above. There are isolated records of dolls' houses having been made for very privileged little girls as early as the middle of the sixteenth century. A detailed inventory exists of the contents of such a doll's house made in 1558 for the daughter of Duke Albrecht of Saxony, and it is not improbable that similar houses, complete with fixtures and furnishings, were manufactured in Nuremberg about the same time, though none has survived that can definitely be attributed to that period.

Several examples of dolls' houses dating from about 1600 have been preserved in museum collections. At an early stage the familiar style was beginning to emerge in the form of a model house with its façade consisting of a hinged door opening to reveal the rooms in section. Others, however, were closer to the traditional display cabinet, with a glass front covering what is essentially a box divided into compartments, each devoted to the furnishings associated with a different room in the house. The majority of the dolls' houses – or 'baby-houses' as they were then known – were playthings for ladies rather than little girls and the extravagance lavished on many of these houses is well documented. In general the more expensive furnishings are associated with the cabinets produced in France and the Low Countries, whereas the homelier items, designed for dolls' houses that resembled the real thing, were a German speciality. At first the English tended to follow the example of the Dutch, but by the early years of the eighteenth century some attractive baby-houses were being made for children rather than grown-ups. These beautiful houses were often made locally to the specification of the purchaser and a fine conceit of the period was to have the doll's house modelled on one's own residence. This charming custom declined in the nineteenth century, but has been revived in recent years.

The great majority of Victorian dolls' houses were commercially manufactured and lack the architectural detail and charm of the earlier examples, but what they may have missed in external originality was balanced by the ingenuity lavished on their arrangement and furnishing. A lifetime might be spent on garnering the furniture, the ornaments and bric-à-brac to go inside them, on the carpets and the special miniaturized drapes and wall-hangings. Tiny paintings were cannibalized from the lids of snuff boxes and étuis originally produced as Battersea enamels, or the hand-painted ivory panels from eighteenth-century étuis and bonbonnières, but by the late nineteenth century it was more fun to cut out the decorative vignettes and tail-pieces from books and colour them by hand. Suitably varnished and fitted with a tiny gilt frame, these pictures looked astonishingly realistic.

The best dolls' furniture was hand-made using the finest materials – tables of walnut or mahogany and chairs intricately upholstered in real plush. By the 1870s, however, an ersatz quality was beginning to creep in, and subsequently one finds chairs and sofas with pins instead of joints, and scraps of leather indifferently glued on to backs and seats. By the turn of the century standards

Doll's house modelled as a villa with conservatory and coach house; English, 1889

had declined even further, and much dolls' furniture from then onward was cast in various metal alloys, principally with a lead base. The lowering in standards paralleled the greater demand for dolls' houses and furniture among the less wealthy classes of society. Dolls' houses were no longer the prerogative of the upper classes, and thanks to the democratization of child's play the cheap, mass-produced dolls' houses and their contents are still comparatively plentiful. In the decade prior to the First World War dolls' houses made of stout pasteboard and hardboard, with painted imitation brickwork and roof tiles, were retailing in the United States for less than a dollar, or about four shillings in sterling of that period. Less robust than their wooden counterparts, these cheap houses have not stood the test of time so well and their celluloid windows, in particular, have cracked and become discoloured, whereas the glass windows of the more expensive houses have generally survived rather better.

Just as houses and furniture might vary considerably in quality, so also the minor fitments ranged from expensive miniatures in glass, porcelain and silver, produced by the craftsmen who worked in these media on full-sized objects, to imitations made in plaster, chalkware or lead alloys respectively. Even these

82

naïve miniatures have a certain primitive charm about them and, in an age where the great bulk of dolls' furniture is made in plastics, they are just as antique in character as the custom-built objects they sought to replace.

Kitchens and shops

Whether dolls' houses were ever intended for the practical instruction of little girls in the household arts is debatable. No such doubt exists concerning the tiny kitchens which were a speciality of the Nuremberg toymakers from the early seventeenth century onwards. It has been argued that many of the so-called 'Nuremberg kitchens' were not German at all but emanated from the Netherlands. Be that as it may, these cabinets, usually about two feet in length and eighteen inches in height, were designed primarily to teach girls housekeeping. The kitchen stove was the central point, and above it were suspended tiny examples of skimmers, ladles and serving-spoons. On racks to left and right were miniature platters and dishes in decorated earthenware, and shelves contained serried ranks of pewter plates and copper pots and pans of all shapes and designs likely to occur in any well-appointed kitchen. Benches and stools were fitted into the sides of the cabinet and miscellaneous items of equipment, from cake moulds to rolling pins, were also set out. Fire irons, flat irons, brooms and dustpans were arrayed around the hearth. The best examples of these model kitchens combined the arts of the metalworker, the potter and the wood-turner. More imaginative examples, likely to have been designed for child's play rather than as a visual aid to domestic science, were produced in Germany, France and England in the late seventeenth and early eighteenth centuries, and rare examples have been recorded as manufactured in the USA and Canada before the end of the eighteenth century. As the nineteenth century progressed toy kitchens became more of a plaything; the objects tend to look unreal and out of proportion, and eventually they ceased to appear as a separate entity, but were merely one room in the standard doll's house. Towards the end of the century kitchen toys began to revive and from then on we find examples of stoves and cookers in tinplate and sets of pots and pans to match; but the original idea of the kitchen, conceived as an entity with complete equipment, was a thing of the past.

Contemporary with the earliest 'Nuremberg kitchens' were similar cabinets designed as shops and, like the kitchens, produced as instructional models rather than as toys. For this reason the commonest form was the butcher's shop with row upon row of assorted joints of meat hanging from hooks. The pieces of meat and even whole carcasses were carved from wood or moulded in plaster, realistically painted to simulate the texture of real meat – blood and all. By looking at these models, rather than playing with them, little girls mastered the different cuts of meat. Model shops, intended for play rather than instruction, developed in the eighteenth century and as well as the butcher's shop (which continued to be a firm favourite) one finds bakeries, greengrocers' and grocers'

Above Toy kitchen;
American (probably New
York), late 18th century

Below Toy kitchen stove
(7 in high); English,
c 1900

shops. Less frequently met with are the clothes' shops or *modistes* which, understandably, were mostly of French origin. Toy shops consisted of long cabinets divided horizontally to provide a shop counter on which stood scales, display stands and other equipment associated with each type of shop. The goods themselves were arranged on shelves at the back and sides, or suspended from racks as the case might be. The earlier examples of toy shops relied heavily on plaster imitations of fruit, vegetables and other grocery items, though tiny glass bottles and exquisitely formed wooden boxes showed the lengths to which the toymakers would go in attempting realism. The toy grocer's shop was revolutionized, however, when American manufacturers hit upon the idea of using it as a medium for advertising branded goods which were produced in miniature packs, tins and bottles for this purpose. The idea probably developed out of the miniature samples which salesmen carried around the country to prospective customers. The earliest examples of these packages, dating from the 1870s, were plaster dummies, but at the beginning of this century miniaturized packs of real goods were used. This practice flourished for about twenty years and then deciined after the First World War, though it has survived sporadically to this day in both America and Europe.

Like the toy kitchens, the toy shops of more recent times have not been confined to a single cabinet built for that express purpose. Toy-shop kits began to appear at the turn of the century, paralleling the separate stoves and kitchen sets. The components of these kits were generally much larger than those in the

Toy grocer's shop; German, *c.* 1880

earlier model shops (which were only meant to be looked at), and this reflects the new emphasis in such toys, which were meant to be handled. From this period date the sets of toy money, both coins and banknotes, which could be used in toy-shop transactions. Sets of toy money were also sold separately and were an invaluable aid to teaching children arithmetic in a painless manner. The early coins were made of bronze, brass or white metal simulating the gold and silver then in use.

From the beginning of this century also the range of shops increased enormously and took in banks, filling stations, railway booking offices and post offices, complete with special equipment, rubber stamps and stationery. Toy stamps, usually about a quarter of the real thing in size, often imitated the colours, denominations and inscriptions of stamps then current, and examples of these are of great interest to philatelists. Others were completely (and deliberately) unrealistic, with inscriptions of fantasy countries such as Fairyland, Toyland or Toytown. This has not precluded their actual use on occasion by young children, especially on letters to Santa Claus dropped into mailboxes. Postally used examples of these toy stamps on cover are not uncommon, but can be regarded as little more than curiosities.

The earliest of these composite models aimed at little boys also had a didactic motif, but they are much rarer than the kitchens and butchers' shops, probably because boys were sooner introduced to the real thing. Examples of toy stables, complete with model carts and horses and saddlery, date from the late eighteenth century and are seldom met with. In the nineteenth century, however, toy farmyards became popular and survive to this day, having undergone tremendous changes as the technology of farming and husbandry have altered and been modernized. Farm animals were hand-carved in wood, and numerous examples have been recorded from southern Germany and the Tyrol from medieval times onward. Tin or lead alloy models of cattle, dogs, sheep and farm workers parallel the developments in model soldiers (see below), but plaster and papier mâché were also used at different times in producing farmyard models. Analogous to the farmyard was the Noah's ark, whose animals, in pairs of course, covered the entire range of zoology. The arks themselves were little more than a receptacle for the model animals and birds and are usually fairly crude affairs, consisting of square, box-like houses set in the wooden hull of a boat. The roofs usually lift off to reveal a cabinet wherein the animals and Noah's family can be stored. The ark was not integral to the play itself, since the idea was to set out the animals in their pairs, according to orders and species, in the form of a procession or grouped around the ark. Arks of this type were made from the sixteenth century at least and reached the height of their popularity in the nineteenth century, when they were manufactured in many different forms on both sides of the Atlantic. The animals vary considerably, both in manufacture and in type, ranging from the cheaper models, containing only the basic farmyard animals and a few elephants and giraffes for good measure, to the most exotic sets incorporating

Opposite A dolls' tea party in the Children's Room of the Roger Morris-Jumel Mansion, New York City

Left Noah's ark and set of
carved wooden animals;
German, mid-19th century

literally hundreds of species from the ends of the earth. The better examples
were hand-carved and painted, and this continued to be a speciality of the
German toymakers, though increasingly cast-lead models were used. Model
fire stations and railway stations, with their distinctive vehicles and rolling-
stock as well as model personnel, are a late nineteenth-century development
from the toy forts discussed below.

Model soldiers and martial toys

By long-established tradition boys have played with model soldiers, forts and
cannon, while girls have played with dolls. Model soldiers for boys' games date
back to ancient Egypt and, nearer the present day, there are numerous
accounts of kings and generals, both men and boys, who have played with such
toys. From Louis XIV to Sir Winston Churchill and H. G. Wells, famous men
have indulged their passion for model soldiers and countless small boys have
collected them avidly over the past three hundred years. Today the collecting
of model soldiers and the science of carpet strategy have become respectable
adult pursuits under the names of *Kriegspiel* or war-gaming, and this has led to
the revival of finely executed models in metal alloys, at a time when plastics
have captured the mass market. Even the cheap lead or 'tin' soldiers of
yesteryear have now become desirable antiques, especially if preserved with
the original manufacturer's box.

Opposite Group of toys for
boys: hansom cab and
horseless carriage made of
cardboard, *c.* 1900; wooden
soldiers, *c.* 1860, and a gun
and gun team

89

Though models of soldiers have been made in ivory, wood, pottery and even precious metals for over two thousand years, the hobby only became widespread in the eighteenth century and was largely inspired by the military exploits of Frederick the Great, himself a keen devotee of model soldiers. The manufacture of these models was transformed from a craft to an industry by the Hilpert family, working first in Nuremberg and latterly in Coburg. By the end of the century, however, *zinnsoldaten* (tin soldiers, usually made of tin or a pewter alloy) were being produced in many parts of Germany, catering to a vast export market. The early soldiers were 'flats' – two-dimensional figures mounted on a small metal stand, which was often impressed with the initials or even the full name of the maker. At first there was no attempt at standardization and soldiers might range from an inch to four inches in height. Some degree of uniformity was established in the mid-nineteenth century by Heinrichsen, whose Nuremberg scale of 30 mm for a figure was soon adopted by most other manufacturers.

Although the German manufacturers dominated the market in the nineteenth century, soldiers were made in France, Italy, Scandinavia and even in England, and materials other than tin were also used. Model soldiers, somewhat larger than the Nuremberg figures, may be found in wood, papier mâché, chalkware and stout card, but they were never as satisfactory as the metal soldiers and gradually died out. Eventually toymakers outside Germany

Scottish baronial-style infantry barracks and parade ground

Field ambulance set by
William Britain, 1906

began making metal soldiers themselves and in many ways improved on the technique. The French were probably the first to produce models with a three-dimensional appearance, but these solid-cast figures were rather expensive and this led William Britain of London to devise a process for hollow-casting, which not only permitted greater realism but was more economic in terms of materials. Three-dimensional figures were also made in Germany by Heyde of Dresden, mainly for export since German collectors continued to prefer 'flats'. By the end of the century several German manufacturers had mastered Britain's hollow-casting process and were producing soldiers of this type. Nevertheless, Britain's lead soldiers were in a class of their own and those produced between 1893 and 1914 rank among the more expensive collectors' pieces today, particularly the sets, such as the balloon team, pontoon-bridge unit and the horse artillery gun crew.

The model soldiers of the United States were often home-produced in paper, card, plaster or metal alloys, but the majority of the soldiers of the nineteenth century were imported from Germany. The Eureka Company began producing good quality metal soldiers in 1898 and from then onward German imports lost ground. The First World War drastically hit the German model-soldier industry, but long before that time the manufacture of tin or lead soldiers was well established in most western countries and the industry had even become established in Japan. To some extent Japan captured the market for cheap metal soldiers in the 20s, but the quality market continued to be dominated by such internationally famous companies as Heyde, Britain, Beiser of the United States and Mignot of Paris.

The manufacturers of model soldiers also produced their weapons and other equipment. Many of the carriages and cannon produced by the German makers were 'flats' like the soldiers and were entirely non-functional, but by the 1870s they were bowing to the demand for carriages whose wheels would actually turn and cannon with spring-loaded barrels which would fire a pellet. As *Kriegspiel* increased in popularity, and was finally codified in Wells' classic *Little Wars*, the need for more realistic and effective cannon increased. On the eve of the First World War a prodigious variety of artillery was available to the war-gamer, using ammunition that ranged from tiny steel darts to wooden shells. Toy forts served a dual purpose, both ornamental and useful. They provided an impressive focal point to a display of model soldiers, but were often designed as receptacles in which the soldiers could be packed away at the end of the day. The commercially manufactured forts were generally rather plain in appearance. Like dolls' houses, however, the more expensive ones were often hand-made by a local carpenter, with a bewildering complexity of towers and vedettes, drawbridges, portcullis and crenellated battlements, all mixed together in a glorious confusion of styles drawn from the military architecture of the past thousand years. With the First World War, however, came the vogue for such grim accessories as tiny barbed wire entanglements and walls of sand-bags (the latter often cast in metal and painted to resemble the real thing), machine-gun nests and the ultimate weapon of the age – the tank, either of solid wood or tinplate construction.

Dolls' costume and accessories

Dolls' clothing is a subject as vast and as ancient as the dolls themselves and we are here concerned only with dolls' costume and accessories as separate entities. Bearing in mind that the vast majority of dolls' clothes were hand-made, and that the dressing-up was the essence of the play, it is not surprising that this is an enormous field requiring a separate volume to do it justice. The manufacture of clothing and accessories was an important adjunct of doll-making in both Germany and France, especially from the mid-eighteenth century, and it became customary to sell dolls which were not only fully clothed but which were accompanied by trunks containing articles of dress to cover every conceivable occasion – from ball gowns to riding habit – as well as minor articles such as boots and shoes, gloves, parasols and hats. The fashion for dolls' trousseaux and layettes reached its height in the second half of the nineteenth century with the manufacture of special trunks, bandboxes and cases fitted out with sets of clothing for both outer and underwear.

Underclothes received scant attention from the early doll-makers, following the line that the doll was intended as a model for outer wear alone, but as the craze for dressing dolls reached its peak, a much keener interest was paid to

Doll's sewing machine;
English, late 19th century

92

those articles not normally exposed to view. Chemises and petticoats were the earliest examples of underwear to be produced in any quantity. Drawers came rather later, and in fact paralleled their adoption by ladies in polite society from the 1840s onward. By the 1860s, however, highly elaborate doll's corsets were being produced in Europe, with intricate stitching and boning which emulated the real thing. Dolls were forced into stiff, tight-laced training corsets just like their youthful charges, providing yet another example of the way in which dolls were used to teach girls a code of conduct for real life.

Thereafter dolls' dress accessories faithfully reflect contemporary changes in fashion, from the muffs and tippets of outerwear to the bibs and pinafores in everyday use in the nursery. Many examples of late nineteenth-century dolls' underwear were hand-stitched by girls and their mothers, and framed sets of these garments were analogous to the samplers sewn in earlier times – proof that the young lady had attained a certain level of competence with needle and thread that would equip her for one of the most important household chores of that period. Other articles of costume, however, continued to be commercially manufactured, and this industry expanded greatly at the turn of the century. Before the First World War the large department stores in both Europe and America had toy departments retailing a vast range of dress accessories, from hats to shoes, in various sizes to fit the smallest and the largest dolls. After languishing to some extent in the interwar years the market in dress accessories for dolls revived, though it has now been overtaken by the cult of the dress-up dolls such as Barbie, Sindy and Action Girl, whose outfits for every conceivable occasion provide infinite scope.

Doll's bonnets and parasol; English, mid-late 19th century

93

Articles of dress, other than the delightfully dated sets of underwear mounted and framed, are of little interest in themselves and can only be diaplayed to advantage when fitted to dolls. On the other hand, there are many other kinds of associated accoutrements which are perfectly collectable on their own. Parasols, umbrellas, canes and walking sticks, on the scale of one inch to a foot or smaller, may be found in a great variety of styles, reflecting the range of full-sized articles. Pipes, tobacco pouches and snuff boxes are much scarcer, but are exceedingly attractive miniatures to collect. Purses, bags and reticules in the prevailing styles of the eighteenth and nineteenth centuries are eminently suitable for collecting on their own. Dolls' jewelry is an interesting subject in itself, affording great scope to the collector. Most items were made of glass paste with gilt or white-metal settings, but examples of brooches, rings, pendants and necklaces in gold, using precious or semi-precious stones are not unknown. Tiny earrings incorporating real pearls and necklaces of amber and jet in miniature form were produced for dolls' wear from the early nineteenth century onwards.

Dolls' crockery and cutlery

An important part of the doll ritual, then as now, consisted of feeding-time, interpreted variously in different countries. From the early nineteenth century onwards there were many books published in Europe and Britain which read rather like the etiquette books aimed at adults bent on improving themselves.

Miniature cups and saucers featuring Queen Alexandra (*c.* 1902), Felix the Cat, Beatrix Potter characters and Kate Greenaway figures; English, early 20th century

These little books gave the rules of doll-play, but were a not too subtle hint aimed at the girls themselves. In suggesting do's and don'ts to the youthful 'mama' on the manners and behaviour of her inanimate charges, the publishers of these books no doubt felt that they were performing a useful service. The best way to instil good manners into a little girl was to let her teach them to her dolls. Thus table manners were more than fully covered in the instructions for giving dolls their breakfast, afternoon tea or supper, with notes on what was good and bad for their diet.

Apart from the very small services of china intended as part of the furniture of dolls' houses, and the earlier platters associated with Nuremberg kitchens and the like, larger examples of crockery were produced by the majority of the potteries in the nineteenth century as a sideline to their normal output. A few, very expensive tea and dinner services were manufactured in porcelain with hand-painted motifs, but most of them were transfer-printed in underglaze blue, the Chinese 'willow pattern' being the commonest design. Towards the end of the century the variety of designs in dolls' crockery widened to include transfer prints of nursery characters, while contemporary scenes and figures of children in everyday garb and situations became very popular in the 1890s. Thereafter dolls' crockery tended to follow the same patterns and styling found in full-sized services. Elaborate sets in hardpaste porcelain, bone china, ironstone and earthenware continued to cater to all sections of the market up to the time of the Second World War, but since then ceramics have been largely superseded by plastics, which have the dubious merit of being unbreakable. It is unlikely that the modern utilitarian services, with their streamlined styling, will ever match the charm of the teasets in traditional materials.

Cutlery for use at dolls' tea parties varied considerably in quality, the commonest type being rather roughly die-stamped from pewter sheet. The lower end of the market is satisfied nowadays by the use of plastics, though occasionally aluminium alloys are employed. The best of dolls' cutlery appeared at the turn of the century, and took the form of tiny knives, forks and spoons in electroplate with handles of wood, ivory or bone. Tiny spoons which had a very real usage, such as salt or mustard spoons, could be pressed into dolls' service and have caused some confusion amongst collectors generations later, but there can be no mistake regarding the little knives and forks, seldom more than two inches in length and often much smaller, which were designed by the cutlers of London, Birmingham, Sheffield or Solingen and exported all over the world. The knives invariably have rounded ends and no cutting edge; nothing was allowed to obtrude into the world of make-believe that might have caused an unfortunate accident in the nursery. Individual examples of dolls' cutlery are not scarce, but complete canteens of cutlery are decidedly rare.

6 Visual Entertainment

Many mothers of the present day have good reason to bless the memory of John Logie Baird for his gift of television to mankind. It has become all too easy nowadays to keep children out of mischief by setting them down in front of a television set. The nannies and nursemaids of yesteryear might be horrified at the stooping posture of many modern children and that glazed, far-away look born of too much viewing – not to mention their utter contempt for TV dinners and their possibly deleterious effects on the juvenile appetite. Be that as it may, the seeds of today's passive entertainment were sown a long time ago, and the Victorian child had a wide range of visual amusements to choose from and they were doubtless just as spell-binding and enchanting in their way as *Skippy, The Magic Roundabout* or the Hannah-Barbera cartoons.

Toy theatres

The rise in popularity of the theatre in Europe in the eighteenth century was reflected in the passion for tableaux, which were produced in Germany and Austria from about 1770 onwards. Like many of the dolls' houses with which they were contemporaneous, these tableaux were designed for adult appreciation rather than the amusement of children. They were large, open-fronted cabinets, often ornately decorated to resemble the neoclassical features fashionable in real theatres of that time. The sides tapered slightly towards the back to create the illusion of depth, and other techniques of perspective heightened the effects of a real theatre. To match these miniature theatres, sheets of hand-coloured engravings were produced and pasted on wood to imitate 'flats', the backdrops and scenery associated with popular drama. The *dramatis personae* of these tableaux consisted of cardboard figures mounted on small wooden stands. Here again, the artists of Vienna and Augsburg published sheets featuring characters from various plays, and these could be coloured, cut out, mounted on wood and put on the stage.

Toy theatres as such originated in England at a rather later date, probably in the first decade of the nineteenth century. Although they probably derived much of their inspiration from Continental tableaux, the English version could also trace its origins back to the theatrical prints which became fashionable in the mid-eighteenth century. The evolution of these theatrical prints was closely

Opposite Pollock's toy theatre, complete with flats and footlights; English, *c.* 1850

97

connected with the development of the English toy theatre, or Juvenile Drama as it is better known. In 1811 there was a subtle change in the layout of these theatrical prints, four small full-length portraits being substituted for the single large portrait hitherto fashionable. The portraits would be of actors and actresses in the costumes associated with a particular play, whose title and principal roles would be given in the captions. This, in turn, developed into sheets featuring six characters from a play, and then to two or more sheets in a series, so that all the *dramatis personae* could be shown. Subsequently, more elaborate sheets were published, covering not only the characters, but changes of costume and scenery within a single production; and, finally, such sheets were published with an accompanying text. These progressive stages took place between 1810 and 1820, and over the ensuing decades Juvenile Drama, as it became known, was a highly popular pastime with adults and children alike. Stevenson's essay on *Penny Plain, Twopence Coloured* evokes the atmosphere of these theatrical sheets. A great deal of skill and artistry was lavished on their production, from the copperplate engraving to the cunning use of three colour combinations to achieve a wide variety of shades.

These toy sheets are believed to have been collected and preserved intact. As such they always had great appeal to adult collectors, though very few sets have survived in pristine condition. Many of them were brought for or by children, to be cut up and used in conjunction with toy theatres. The sheets reflected the fashions in drama of the early nineteenth century, with the accent on Melodrama and pantomimes, but also including more serious works and the plays of Shakespeare. The most prolific publisher of toy sheets was Matthew Skelt, whose imprint may be found on many of the earlier theatrical prints as well. Other publishers included H. J. Webb and Benjamin Pollock, the latter carrying on the tradition of the Juvenile Drama long after others had given it up. Although the heyday of the toy theatre was the first half of the nineteenth century, it survived in a debased form well into the present century and, thanks to the activities of Pollock's Toy Museum in London's Bloomsbury, the traditions of Juvenile Drama were never allowed to disappear entirely, but have in fact been revived in more recent years. The best of Juvenile Drama retains its period flavour and little attempt has been made to inject a contemporary note. The decline of the toy theatre has been explained by the competition from other forms of visual entertainment, culminating in motion pictures and television, which gave children a much more sophisticated attitude towards drama than the melodramatic stage productions of the nineteenth century. Perhaps, also, the toy theatres themselves accelerated their decline. As the century progressed the original toy sheets tended to give way to chromolithographed sheets on glossy card, with the characters and scenery embossed and die-stamped in order to reduce to a bare minimum the effort on the part of the young 'producer'. Personal involvement was always a strong point of the Juvenile Drama and when this was minimized interest was bound to decline.

WEBB'S CHARACTERS IN ALADDIN.

Plate 6

For Sc.5th   *Officer*   *Aladdin*   *Karar Banjou*   *Abanazar*

Tartar Guards   *Officer*   *Tahi Tongluck*   *Officer*   *Widow Mustapha*

London, Pub by W.WEBB, 146, Old Street, St Luke's

Optical toys

Uncut sheets of characters in 'Aladdin' by W. Webb of London, mid-19th century

The insatiable curiosity of children, coupled with their powerful imaginative instinct, was both stimulated and assuaged by peep-shows. Some highly sophisticated examples, their interiors magnified and illuminated, are retailed at the present day, but in essence the peep-show has varied little since its invention by Alberti in Renaissance Italy. The basic peep-show consisted of a box with a tiny aperture in the front and some form of illumination at the back (often no more than a glass panel at the rear, through which daylight could pass). The inside of the box was painted to simulate scenery, and glass panels were inserted from side to side, with their surfaces painted in such a way that the images overlapped or were seen in three-dimensional form. There were numerous variations, but the basic principle remained the same. Peep-shows and dioramas were immensely popular in the nineteenth century, not only as a children's toy but as a public spectacle in fairs and exhibitions; and they also

99

had more serious applications, being used extensively as a technique of salesmanship. The use of mirrors to create reflected images on the same principle as the camera obscura added a new dimension to the peep-show. A variation of the simple peep-show was the telescopic or perspective toy, consisting of a long narrow box or cylinder, with scenery and figure groups arranged at right angles to the sides. The show was viewed through an aperture at one end and the effect conveyed was one of immense distance. The inauguration of the Thames Tunnel about 1840 was commemorated by perspective toys, and similar examples a decade later featured the main hall of the Great Exhibition.

Tiny versions of the peep-show were known as peep-eggs from their characteristic shape. These devices, made of wood, papier mâché or alabaster, contained two scenes viewed through a double-convex lens. These peep-eggs seem to have concentrated on geographical subjects, though biblical tableaux were also popular. The main drawback about peep-shows was their immobility, and children soon tired of looking at the same scene, no matter how elaborate it might be. This problem was overcome by using small glass slides, arranged round the sides of a drum or the periphery of a disc. By rotating a handle, the different images could be viewed one after the other. The variety

Perspective toy depicting the Great Exhibition of 1851

Myriopticon featuring a naval battle of the American Civil War, by Milton Bradley of Springfield, Mass., 1866

of pictures compensated for the lack of depth, which was an important feature of the static peep-shows, and a sequence of images could be used to tell a story or, more probably, to develop the geography lesson. By the end of the nineteenth century rotary viewers of this type were available with a wide range of interchangeable discs or drums. The advent of motion pictures revolutionized this toy, since small film strips could be used instead of glass slides, and this led to the more compact viewers of the 1920s and later years.

Still pictures are probably more acceptable today than they were a century ago, and there is no need for the modern equivalent of the peep-show to compete with television or the movies. In the nineteenth century, however, motion pictures were an unrealized ambition and many of the optical toys then popular attempted to supply a satisfactory substitute. The electronic scanner of television and the moving frames of the cinema both depend on an optical phenomenon known as the persistence of vision. Though known to the ancient Greeks it was not scientifically explained until 1824, when John Ayrton Paris demonstrated its properties to the Royal Society. In his experiments he made use of cardboard discs with pictures of objects on either side. Strings attached to the edges of the disc were twisted between fingers and thumbs so that the disc was made to rotate rapidly. Onlookers observed that the image on one side of the disc became superimposed on the image from the other side. The rotation of the disc also produced the illusion of movement in the objects depicted. The following year Paris patented his discs under the name of a 'Thaumatropical Amusement', and boxes of these discs sold like hot cakes. The Thaumatrope (which may loosely be translated as 'the turning marvel') was the first of a long line of optical toys with complex, pseudo-scientific names derived from Greek.

In 1832 the Austrian, Stampfer, and the Belgian, Plateau, both invented an optical device independently of each other and called their inventions the Strotoscope and the Phenakistiscope respectively (or literally 'spindle viewer' and 'apparition-box-viewer'). These objects consisted of a large cardboard disc with narrow slots cut round the circumference near the edge. Between the slots were pictures of objects differing slightly from each other. Attached to the disc

was a handle of bone or wood, which was used to rotate the disc quickly. The
viewer stood before a mirror and looked at the reflection of the disc through the
slots. The rotation of the disc gave the images the appearance of movement.
The simplicity and effectiveness of this device made it a popular toy, and it was
marketed all over Europe, the USA and Canada under various names, such as
the Magic Disc, the Phantasmascope or the Kaleidorama, and in such guises it
remained a firm favourite for more than sixty years.

The snag about the Phenakistiscope and its brethren was that they could be
used by only one viewer at a time. Curiously enough, a more advanced device
which would permit simultaneous viewing by several people was invented by
W. H. Horn of Bristol about the same time under the name of the Daedalum or
Wheel of Life, but he did nothing to develop it commercially and it was left to
others, in France and the United States, to turn it into a practical proposition
under the name of the Zoetrope. It consisted of a metal drum, revolving on a
spindle attached to a heavy wooden base. A paper strip, half the height of the
drum, was attached to the inside and bore a series of images differing slightly in
a sequence of actions. The drum was rotated and the audience, grouped
around it, viewed the moving images through vertical slits in the side of the
drum. Picture strips were sold in sets and examples of these are still reasonably
plentiful, although the original Zoetropes themselves are scarce.

The Zoetrope was crude compared with the Praxinoscope developed about
a decade later and remaining popular from the 1870s till the beginning of the
twentieth century. This was a much more elaborate affair consisting of a drum
with glass slides featuring objects in a sequence of movements. The drum was
rotated in a box, the inside of whose lid depicted scenery or some other static

background. The movement of the images on the drum was reflected against the background by means of a mirror. Towards the end of the century more sophisticated viewers were developed in the United States, France and Britain—the Tachyscope, which used real photographs for the first time, the Kittiscope, the Kinetescope, the Kinora and the Chromotrope, whose coloured pictures turned over rapidly like flicking through the pages of a book. The last-named was developed commercially in such popular fairground peep-shows as 'What the Butler Saw'.

Although not an animated peep-show in the strict sense, the Kaleidoscope was a popular toy in the nineteenth century and has continued to fascinate children down to the present time. Invented by Sir David Brewster in 1817, this three-sided tube containing small pieces of glass of different colours and shapes has varied little over the years. Mirrors on the inner sides of the tube were angled in such a way that the pieces of glass would form an intricate pattern every time they were shaken up. The serious aspect of the Kaleidoscope—to provide artists and designers with a multiplicity of non-figurative motifs—was soon forgotten because of the limitations of the device, but it has been a perennial favourite with children ever since. Variation lies mainly in the decorative treatment of the triangular case, which is often found with trade names and advertisements in fancy script or childhood scenes and fairy-tale characters.

Magic lanterns and projectors

The dramatic advances in the science of optics in the first half of the nineteenth century transformed the visual entertainment scene from solitary to mass viewing. The earliest forms of projector relied on arrangements of mirrors and were derived from the camera obscura of the fifteenth century. By the beginning of the nineteenth century various devices had been patented which would transmit the image of a picture or the page of a book on to a wall or screen by means of mirrors. The Optique, popular in France from about 1790 onwards, was the ancestor of the Epidiascope, used to this day as a visual aid in instruction. Most of these contraptions, however, were exceedingly clumsy and were probably too complicated for children to operate successfully.

Experiments with lenses and lighting to beam a picture from a transparent slide took place about the same time, and primitive magic lanterns had begun to appear before the end of the eighteenth century. The image they cast was so fuzzy and distorted that they had little practical application, and were regarded merely as a childish curiosity. Once the problems of focus and parallax had been located and overcome, however, the magic lantern was transformed from an idle curiosity into a serious educational aid with an instant appeal to those bent on improving the minds of the young. By the middle of the nineteenth century the magic lantern was as well established in Europe and America as television is today—though confined, of course, to the

Above Projecting
Phenakistiscope,
incorporating a magic
lantern and moving
pictures, *c.* 1870

Right The Kinora, in which
pictures are flicked over
rapidly to convey
movement; English, late
19th century

better class of household. Magic lanterns came in all shapes and sizes, from the diminutive hand-held projectors and attachments for domestic oil-lamps to the enormous machines (complete with smoke-stack!) employed at public meetings. The small magic lanterns used in nursery picture-shows came in a wide range of designs, few of which were strictly functional. With their metal cases either brightly enamelled or embossed and gilded with pictorial motifs they were regarded as a suitable ornament for the drawing room as well as the nursery. The more expensive models were housed in mahogany cases with much gleaming brasswork. Often the boxes for the glass slides were embellished with matching decoration. Since the slides were large – up to three inches square in many instances – their storage presented a problem, and beautiful cabinets were constructed to hold trays of sets which might each consist of a hundred or more slides.

If the magic lanterns themselves are too cumbersome to be collected in large numbers, the glass slides are a more practical proposition. Slides vary in size from less than an inch square to the standard lecture size of four inches. As well as single slides there were multiples, of French and German manufacture, which foreshadowed the modern filmstrip by having four or five frames on a single sheet of glass measuring about $1\frac{1}{2}$ by 7 inches, and there were similar elongated slides with a single panoramic view instead of isolated frames; by moving these long slides through the lantern, the effect of 'panning' from left to right was achieved. There were rotary slides, consisting of circular pieces of glass with portraits or scenic views on the periphery. As the slide revolved, successive images passed before the lenses and were beamed on to the screen. Although glass was the commonest substance used, celluloid and similar transparent substances were used increasingly from 1860 onwards, stiffened by cardboard mounts in the same fashion as modern transparencies. From the collector's viewpoint, however, these slides are less satisfactory since most of them have become distorted or cracked with age.

Slides were sold in sets containing anything from eight to a hundred, dealing with a specific subject and usually accompanied by a leaflet or booklet providing a commentary. The range of subjects available by the end of the nineteenth century was almost infinite. Geography, history and religious subjects predominated, but botany, zoology and countless aspects of the sciences also had their fair share. Here again, the didactic element was all-pervasive, though a good proportion of slides were of a more frivolous character. Where the emphasis was laid on entertainment, various trick effects were provided in an attempt to simulate movement. Animation was achieved by the use of cogs and levers attached to the projector mechanism so that the slide could be made to jump up and down or slip from side to side rapidly. The image on the screen could thus be made to move rapidly and the old trick of persistence of vision did the rest.

7 Musical Instruments

Because home entertainment was very important in an era before the advent of radio and television the musical aspect of a child's education was stressed heavily and both boys and girls were expected to be proficient in one or more musical instruments. Even in the poorer households the badge of respectability, for all to see, was the piano in the front room. Although the piano was universally accepted as *the* instrument, a surprisingly wide range of other musical instruments was popular in the nineteenth century. Stringed instruments in particular came in a much greater variety than they do today. The banjo and ukelele, imported to Europe from the United States and based on Negro and Hawaiian originals, were both much more popular than they are today, but Europe could produce a host of instruments derived from the medieval lute, from the mandolin to the guitar. Harp derivatives, from the zither to the all but forgotten ophicleide, were also immensely popular. Wind instruments were perhaps less favoured, though fifes, flutes, recorders and piccolos had their adherents. Of the orchestral instruments, the violin and viola were firm favourites, second only to the piano for domestic music-making. Horns of various kinds were less popular on account of their nuisance value, but trombones, saxophones, clarinets and oboes occasionally added variety to musical soirées.

Rattles, bells and drums

The urge to make a noise is one of the basic instincts of the youngest children. As soon as he is old enough to grasp a rattle, a baby will derive obvious pleasure from shaking it vigorously, while the cacophony of a rattle, wielded by mother or nanny, would often pacify the most fractious infant. If 'musical instruments' is interpreted in its widest sense, rattles would certainly qualify; from the apparently monotonous sound the infant picks up the elements of rhythm. Rattles have been found the world over from the earliest times, from calabashes and gourds containing pebbles to the exquisite silver toys of the eighteenth century. From the seventeenth century onwards more complex rattles were produced in many parts of Europe, incorporating tiny bells and hollow handles with mouth-pieces which would produce a musical whistle. These rattles often had a coral handle which also served as a teething ring. Many of the rattles of

Silver rattle with coral handle; American, mid-19th century

Opposite Tambourine with painted face, ribbons and bells; English, *c.* 1900

107

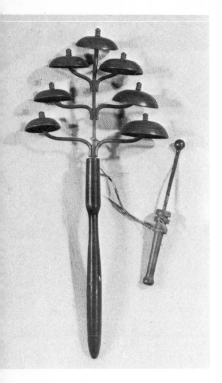

Set of seven musical bells;
English, late 19th century

the late nineteenth century were produced in fancy shapes simulating animal or human figures, but others of a more functional appearance were designed primarily as musical instruments, like maraccas, which could be rattled rhythmically as accompaniment to stringed or wind instruments.

More melodious than rattles, bells were also used for centuries as a means of pacifying or distracting fretful children, but their musical qualities were developed from the eighteenth century onward. Sets of hand-bells with different tones became popular in Europe, played by groups of children each armed with a pair of bells, but about the same time wood and wire frames containing sets of small bells became popular. The German *Glockenspiel* (literally 'bell game') was adapted in many forms suitable for children.

Undoubtedly the most popular and most ancient form of juvenile musical instrument was the drum. Hollow pieces of wood or animal skins stretched tightly over a cylindrical framework have been used by mankind from the earliest times. Although few early examples of drums have survived, there is an abundance of pictorial record to show that drums were used as playthings in ancient Greece and in China more than two thousand years ago. In medieval woodcuts and the pictorial embellishment of illuminated manuscripts children are frequently depicted with drums. In the family portraits of the sixteenth and subsequent centuries the drums held by little boys became more and more sophisticated, miniature versions of the side-drums and tenor-drums used in European armies of the period. Tinware drums ousted the traditional construction in the juvenile market early in the nineteenth century, but gradually 'skins' re-asserted themselves. A tin drum was adequate for a toddler intent merely on making a loud noise, but nothing could surpass a proper drum for resonance and tone. Since then the two types of toy drum have existed side by side, satisfying the demands of the infantile and more advanced sections of the market respectively. Their interest lies mainly in the decoration round the sides, ranging from heraldry to hunting and martial scenes.

Less widespread, but also popular from the middle of the nineteenth century onwards, were tambourines which combined the percussion element of drums with tiny bells. They may be found in a large variety of materials, from the parchment and wooden frames of the traditional designs, to tinplate and stout cardboard of the present century. Because their sides were much narrower, tambourines afforded much less scope for pictorial treatment, yet quite a wide variety of styles and motifs may be encountered. Toy cymbals and gongs were also fashionable at the end of the nineteenth century, but as their surfaces were left undecorated, there is much less scope for the collector looking for distinctive varieties.

Stringed instruments

Probably the most fascinating group of musical toys are those which emulate the adult versions of stringed instruments. At first these were merely scaled

108

down to suit the requirements of children's hands and fingers and had the same skill and craftsmanship lavished on them as the full-sized instruments. Tiny violins and guitars, made of proper materials to traditional specifications, are known to have been made from the fifteenth century onwards and most of them are of considerable rarity and value. Miniature violins are made to this day, and the value of the more modern examples will depend to a large extent on the quality and tone of the instrument.

In the second half of the nineteenth century, however, small violins and guitars began to appear on the market intended purely as toys, without the same consideration being given to virtuosity and tonal qualities. These toy instruments could produce a few notes–after a fashion. Toy banjos and ukeleles were produced in large quantities at the turn of the century, when these instruments were at the height of their popularity. These toys vary considerably in quality from those that merely produced a twanging noise to the few which attempted to produce the right sounds. The better examples were made of wood, but others were produced in composition materials, such as papier mâché or even in tinware. The cheaper examples were gaudily embellished with the usual nursery motifs, so there is unlikely to be any doubt as to their true nature.

Somewhat more advanced were the numerous board instruments of the same period. Of these the zither was the most popular and there are many examples, based on the traditional instrument of Central Europe, which were competently strung and produced a proper sequence of notes, even if the timbre of the adult version was lacking. The majority of these late nineteenth-century zithers had plain black or brown boards, occasionally decorated with floral motifs, though a few may be found in pastel shades with fairy-tale vignettes. Toy harps and lyres of the late nineteenth century were probably a manifestation of the Romantic Revival, but they never achieved any degree of popularity.

Mouth instruments

This term is used because many toy musical instruments were not strictly of the wind variety but were nevertheless played with the mouth. A good example of the latter is the Jew's harp, whose basic design and method of playing have remained unaltered for centuries. Known as the Jew's trump in the Middle Ages, its present name is something of a misnomer. More correctly it should be known as a jaw's harp, since the notes are produced by the action of the player's jaws, opening and closing the mouth to vary the pitch and tone of the vibrations set up by twanging the spring-like attachment at the base of the harp. Wrought iron was mainly used in the production of Jew's harps and they may be found in various sizes, with decorative flourishes on their sides.

Whistles fall into one or other of two categories. The oldest and commonest type consisted of a pipe with a special mouthpiece that produced the musical

Miniature whistles in carved wood and ivory; European, 19th century

note. Peas or other small round objects held in a container near the mouthpiece produced a trilling sound, and the range of notes depended on the number of finger holes on the stem of the pipe. The majority of whistles had no finger holes at all, and were thus very limited in the range of notes they could produce. Whistles of this sort were incorporated in other objects, such novelties being popular from the late nineteenth century. In particular, musical toothbrushes with whistles in their handles were manufactured in Europe and America from about 1880 onwards. In many respects the more interesting type of whistle was the small round object, usually of tinplate, with a central perforation through which the air passed. These small objects were held in the player's mouth and therefore satisfied the oral fixation of small children. Again, the range of notes was very limited, depending entirely on whether one sucked or blew. A copious quantity of saliva helped to achieve a trilling effect. These whistles were often die-stamped in fancy shapes–frogs and birds being common–though plain discs, not unlike the wheels of tinplate toys, were also plentiful. The whistles were usually painted in bright colours but much of the paintwork tended to wear off as the result of the action of teeth and tongue.

More elaborate 'penny whistles' had a series of holes down their length which could produce a full octave and, in the hands of a skilled player, resulted in tolerably tuneful melody. The majority of these whistles, of German, French, Spanish and English manufacture, were produced in tinplate with a brass or enamel finish. Occasionally they were embellished with die-struck ornament, but the majority are quite plain apart from the maker's name.

Whistles of ascending sizes, grouped together like the mythical pipes of Pan, were also popular in the nineteenth century. In the earlier examples each pipe was fashioned separately and then bound together with narrow metal hoops, but by the end of the century sets of pipes were being produced from tinplate sheet, so that the complete instrument was stamped out of upper and lower sheets of metal, soldered at the seams. Another late nineteenth-century novelty was a pipe with a sliding device which varied the pitch and enabled the player to slide up and down the scale with a single breath. Bulbous pipes and whistles, based on traditional styles found in the remoter parts of Europe, also enjoyed fleeting popularity, but the occarina alone seems to have survived for any length of time. These pipes were made of pottery, and had two or three holes which enabled the player to produce a variety of notes. The kazoo, of American origin, was produced in tinplate in vast quantities and satisfied the needs of those who could not master the art of blowing through a penny whistle. The kazoo relied heavily on the player's own voice to produce its distinctive buzzing notes. In essence this simple instrument, evolved by the Negro slaves on the southern plantations, consisted of a slightly bulbous pipe containing a device which had the same effect as humming through paper and comb.

The most popular form of mouth instrument, however, was, and is, the mouth organ. In its original form this small instrument was invented in 1829 by

Sir Charles Wheatstone, who bestowed on it the fanciful name of aeolina. Tiny strips of reed were fitted to the banks of pipes to produce the notes when a current of air passed through them in either direction, hence the characteristic 'blow-suck' action. Rather confusingly, although Wheatstone's name was soon abandoned, the instrument became known as a harmonica, a term applied in the eighteenth century to a short-lived musical instrument consisting of glass bells hit with wooden hammers like a glockenspiel. The mouth organ, invented in England, was subsequently developed by the German toymakers and Hohner became a household name in this context, producing millions of mouth organs in all sizes for export to other parts of the world. In more recent years the mouth organ has acquired a degree of sophistication never dreamed of by its inventor, and it has attained the status of a serious musical instrument, with a growing amount of music composed specially for it. The story of toy instruments is usually one of adult instruments adapted to suit children's purposes; with the harmonica the situation has been reversed.

Carved and painted wooden bird whistle; Bavarian, *c.* 1925

Harmonica by Hohner; German, 19th century

8 Children's Clothing and Accessories

Prior to the nineteenth century children's clothing tended to be no more than miniature versions of adult costume, as an examination of family portraits will reveal. As the individuality of children began to emerge in the nineteenth century, however, the distinctive clothing requirements of children were also recognized. By the end of the century clothing for both sexes had become standardized and has since evolved fairly slowly. The intervening period, however, was one of transition and experiment, often reflecting enormous social changes and some remarkable passing fancies. As a result the children's clothing of the period from 1810 to 1910 afforded more scope and variety than at any other time before or since.

Boys' dress

From the moment of birth both sexes were dressed alike, first in long dresses and frilled caps and later in skirts, petticoats and frilly drawers. At about the age of four or five boys made the sharp transition from dresses to male attire, and it was not until the Edwardian era (1901–10) that toddlers and infants were put into trousers at the earliest. For much of the nineteenth century the feminine element in boys' clothing–particularly those in the wealthier classes–continued to be strong. Even after boys graduated to trousers they often continued to wear a curious frock-like tunic, much bedecked with ribbons and lace frills at the neck and cuff. Jackets for very small boys did not develop before 1850, at a time when the gentleman's frock-coat was also becoming shorter and less elaborate. During the second half of the century a style of jacket emerged with a single button near the neck and no lapels. Trousers were worn uncreased and very tight. Smaller boys wore their trousers on the short side, revealing a generous amount of ankle–a fashion which encouraged a particularly gaudy line in horizontally striped socks. Older boys wore their trousers quite long, without turn-ups, and often having straps which fastened under their boots. Trousers were worn with braces (suspenders) and *never* with a waist-belt. The fashion in men's braces was fanciful and florid and this extended to those worn by boys. The straps were frequently decorated with tiny embroidered motifs, such as dogs and horses, and the metal clips were invariably die-stamped in the prevailing fashion.

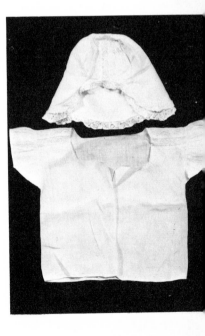

Above Hollie point baby's bonnet and shirt edged in Buckingham lace; English, 17th century

113

Right Lace christening robe; English, 1884

Below Boy's cotton dress suit; English, early 19th century

Footwear underwent several notable changes in the course of the century. At the beginning of the century boys' footwear was closely modelled on that worn by men and consisted mainly of boots which came up to the knee. As the century progressed the height of boys' boots gradually dropped, although there was a revival of high boots in the 1860s. In the early part of the century breeches were tucked into the tops of boots and as the entire length of the boot was visible it was frequently decorated with tassels and a rising front (the so-called Hessian boot) or with a contrasting band of leather at the top (top-boots–often known simply as 'tops'). As trousers became more prevalent boots were concealed by the trouser legs and they therefore became plainer and shorter. Ankle boots for boys came into fashion in the 1840s and were known as high-lows. In general these boots tended to become shorter as the century progressed, apart from a reversal of this trend in the 1870s, when ankle boots with a rising front enjoyed a brief popularity. The term high-lows was eventually extended to ordinary walking shoes, which tended to replace ankle boots towards the end of the century. Nevertheless, ankle boots continued to be worn, particularly by boys of the lower classes, well into the twentieth century.

Indoor slippers, especially those worn by younger children, were made in a wide range of softer materials, both leather and cloth, and often embroidered with fancy patterns.

In the 1870s several distinctive styles of boys' clothing began to emerge, some of them bordering on the extremes of fancy dress, and others of a more practical and lasting quality. Prior to that date the only concession to the whims and caprices of parents was the sailor suit, which became fashionable in the 1840s. It was evolved originally for the elder sons of Queen Victoria, the Prince of Wales and Prince Alfred, who were kitted out in an adaptation of the costume worn by seamen of the Royal Navy. The earliest sailor suits were usually of a white cloth, with bell-bottom trousers, pullover tunic and wide-collared kerchief. This outfit was worn with a broad-brimmed straw hat, of the type then worn by sailors. Anchors, steering wheels and other nautical motifs were embroidered on the breast-pocket of the tunic. The sailor suit underwent several changes later in the century. Though straw hats survived fitfully into the 1920s they were generally superseded by various versions of the flat-topped cap. Trousers lost their bell-bottoms and tended to become shorter. In the 1880s they were even replaced by knickerbockers, mentioned below. After short trousers came into fashion in the early 1900s the sailor suit degenerated into little more than a nautical blouse and cap.

The second romantic fashion of the nineteenth century also began with the British Royal Family. Following the Jacobite Rebellion of 1745–6 the kilt and other articles of Highland dress were proscribed. After a decent interval, however, the ban was lifted, but it was never revived as the everyday garb of the Highlanders. Instead, it was adopted enthusiastically by the nobility and gentry imbued with the romanticism inspired by the novels of Sir Walter Scott, who also masterminded the visit of King George IV to Scotland in 1823, when Highland pageantry was given full rein. The fashion for dressing the sons of the upper classes in kilts and Highland doublets was given tremendous impetus in the 1850s, when Prince Albert purchased Balmoral Castle and the royal children were bedecked in tartan. There was a vogue for tartan materials applied to many articles of dress. The most extravagant ideas on Highland dress found expression in tartan jackets and waistcoats and such articles of headgear as huge feathered hats and fur-laden busbies, but by the 1890s dress had become standardized and Glengarry bonnets came into vogue. Nevertheless, there seemed something incongruous about kilts worn with the short Eton jackets and wide, stiff collars of the period.

If the kilt was the accepted formal dress of the middle- and upper-class boys in Scotland, their counterparts south of the Border fared rather badly. Tunics and breeches of velvet, with lace collar, cuffs and even frills on the breeches, were fashionable from the 1820s onward. This costume was worn with silk stockings, silver-buckled shoes of patent leather and a wide-brimmed hat bedecked with ribbons and feathers. This was known as a Van Dyke suit, from the artist who painted the Court of King Charles I. To complete the

Boy's sailor suit; English, *c.* 1910

Cavalier look, boys were encouraged to grow their hair very long. This was the rig favoured by little Lord Fauntleroy in the novel of the same name by Frances Hodgson Burnett. The book, which was published in 1886 and was immensely popular in Britain and the United States at the turn of the century, led to a marked revival in the Van Dyke style, though it died out during the First World War.

Infinitely more practical, though equally fanciful in its origins, was the knickerbocker suit, which derived its name from the pen-name of Washington Irving, author of the satirical *History of New York*. The baggy breeches, gathered below the knee, as worn by the early Dutch colonists of New Amsterdam, and depicted in Cruikshank's illustrations to the book, gave rise to a new style in trousers. As 'plus fours' they have survived fitfully to this day as the correct apparel for the golf course or the grouse moor. As knickerbockers, usually shortened to knickers, they consisted of loose-fitting breeches gathered just below the knee and worn with knee-length stockings. By the end of the century, however, the knickers worn by boys generally terminated just above the knee, which was left bare. Finally the straps or elastication which kept the leg closed were done away with and the shorts, worn to this day by little boys, came into use.

Girls' dress

The costume worn by girls in the period up to the early nineteenth century generally paralleled that worn by women, but from the 1820s onward the styles of dress worn by adults and children gradually diverged. In general girls' dress followed the pattern of adult clothing, but was simplified and modified in several ways. Though little girls, from the earliest age, were put into tightly-laced corsets, the bodices of girls' costume did not accentuate this fact to the same extent as women's dress. Moreover, while ladies wore their dresses trailing the ground and never revealed so much as their ankles, girls wore frocks which ended at least six inches from the ground. They thus showed their footwear – either ankle boots or flat shoes – a generous length of stocking and the frilled hems of both petticoats and drawers.

The drawers themselves were a recent innovation. Even quite late in the century there were many ladies who did not wear drawers at all, while in many cases these garments consisted only of twin tubes of cambric material, covering the legs and joined to a waistband which provided no cover to the lower part of the abdomen or the seat. By the 1860s, however, drawers had become much more substantial, and were often combined with an under-bodice. Both ordinary drawers and combinations had either an open crotch or an ingenious arrangement, aptly known as a flap. Skirts were bell-shaped or flared, with stiffened petticoats to simulate the effect of the hooped crinolines worn by women between 1856 and 1870. Mercifully, no attempt was made to copy the crinolette or the bustle which were fashionable in the 1870s and 1880s. Instead

Victorian photograph of
two small girls, probably in
party dress

girls' dresses tended to become shorter and simpler. Puffed sleeves became
fashionable in the late 1860s and aprons became larger and longer,
culminating in the pinafore, a sleeveless overall designed to protect dresses in
an age when the laundering of fine materials was often impracticable.
Gradually the pinafore graduated from being a form of bib-apron to a garment
in its own right. The starched white 'pinny' became the most characteristic
female garment at the turn of the century. By 1910, however, it was on the
wane, being superseded by simpler forms of dress in which the gymslip was the
most notable. Drawers and pantalettes became shorter in the 1890s. The
styling of these undergarments became simpler, and elastic replaced the
unreliable waist-buttons and the ribbons at the knee. At the turn of the century
the term 'drawers' was going out of use and the alternatives – knickers or
bloomers – allude respectively to the boys' wear and ladies' sporting dress on
which they were loosely modelled.

Girls' corsetry followed the same lines as the stays worn by women, but was

Above Child's silk tartan dress with black velvet bows, *c.* 1860

Right Girl's coat and cape; English, *c.* 1880

Below Children's shoes, American, 18th-19th centuries, and English fan

generally cut on simpler lines and less severe in effect. Various types of training corset were being marketed in the 1880s and 1890s, with a number of patent devices involving straps and laces which the manufacturers claimed would produce the proper posture, but it is a matter for conjecture how popular these garments were. They were extensively advertised, but few examples appear to have survived. By the beginning of the present century a much simpler and more comfortable garment—the liberty bodice—was becoming established. It enclosed the upper part of the body and was usually buttoned down the middle. Suspenders (American garters) were fitted to the hem to support the stockings.

Little girls were less prone to romantic styles of dress than their brothers. To be sure, there were fanciful costumes incorporating Scottish tartans and floppy Magyar hats which were supposed to be modelled on the headgear of the Hungarian peasants. But the nearest approach to the Lord Fauntleroy suits was the pseudo-Regency style in sack dresses and frilled bonnets popularized in the drawings of Kate Greenaway in the 1880s. The artless shifts, with puffed, short sleeves and frilled hems, embodied the ideals of the Arts and Crafts Movement and the fashion appealed to those Victorians who wanted something simpler than the fussy styles of the period. The Kate Greenaway style died out during the First World War, when much simpler fashions were becoming prevalent anyway, but there have been attempts to revive it in recent years for party or formal wear. Miss Greenaway did much to popularize a style of outer wear for girls, consisting of large hats, fur-trimmed coats and muffs, which became the fashionable Sunday wear for the daughters of the well-to-do in the 1890s. The better quality muffs were made of fur, but there were more decorative examples in quilted satins. The gloves worn by girls were closely modelled on those used by women and are to be found mainly in silk and various types of leather.

Minor dress accessories afford considerable scope for collection and parallel the fashions found in adult dress. Girls' footwear of the nineteenth and early twentieth centuries is relatively plentiful and may be found in an astonishing range of styles and forms. Slippers with satin or brocade tops were often decorated with fancy embroidery or even beadwork. Outdoor wear was robust by modern standards and consisted of sturdy, low-heeled boots terminating at the ankle or extending to the top of the calf. They were secured by innumerable tiny, nail-breaking buttons; later versions incorporated elastic panels in their sides to provide a snug and comfortable fit. Patent-leather pumps and low evening shoes were often decorated with fancy buckles, generally in cut steel, though the more ornamental varieties might be in die-struck silver plate.

Nail file, button hook and buffer from a manicure set with ivory handles carved with heads in the style of Kate Greenaway

LITTLE
WIDE-
AWAKE

400 PICTURES

9 Nursery Literature

Nursery literature, like the nursery itself, reached its height in the last quarter of the nineteenth century. This was the heyday of the moral and improving tale, the exquisite toy books of Walter Crane and the most elegant of the Sunday School prize books. It also witnessed the birth of such disparate literary forms as the boys' adventure stories based on historical facts, pioneered by Henty, the school stories and novels aimed at adolescent girls in the refreshing style of Louisa M. Alcott and the animal stories of Joel Chandler Harris and Beatrix Potter. But children's books evolved gradually over a period of centuries. Until comparatively recently they were virtually ignored by bibliophiles and their true rarity went unrecognized. Bearing in mind the rough usage to which books were often subjected by their youthful owners it is hardly surprising that early editions of nineteenth-century works are scarce, while examples of children's books from earlier periods are among the major rarities of literature.

Children's books existed in Europe long before the invention of printing. Numerous versions of Aesop's *Fables* in manuscript form have been preserved, and some of these date from the Middle Ages. Of comparable antiquity are such works as the *Gesta Romanorum* and the riddles and scholastic exercises of Aelfric and Alcuin. With the advent of printing in the fifteenth century children's books became more common. The majority of the early works were known as courtesy books and consisted of manuals of behaviour aimed at the sons and daughters of the nobility. Full of moral precepts, mixed with practical do's and dont's about nose-picking and table manners, they were designed to make a boy either a 'litel clergeon, seven years of age' or an esquire, 'curteys, lowly and servisable'. More sophisticated books were published in the seventeenth century and ran into many editions. Among the most notable are Francis Osborne's *Advice to a Son* (1656), *A Lady's Gift, or Advice to a Daughter* by the Marquess of Halifax (1688) and the controversial *Letters to his Son* (1774) by the Earl of Chesterfield. The last-named is one of the most sophisticated volumes of its kind, but at the time of publication it was roundly condemned on grounds of immorality and provoked a spate of puritanical antidotes. The Puritans in England and America in the seventeenth century produced many books written for children as children, not as miniature adults, and without the insistence on the acquisition of social graces, which characterized the earlier

Opposite Little Wide-Awake, cover designed by Kate Greenaway, 1880

books. The majority of these Puritan books were fiercely moral textbooks which established a tradition in children's literature for the grim and horrific, the dire punishments for idleness and immorality. Yet it was a Puritan writer who first appreciated that children needed something less stark. In 1686 the first edition of John Bunyan's *Book for Boys and Girls; or, Country Rhimes for Children* appeared. Later published under the shorter title of *Divine Emblems*, it remained very popular until the beginning of the nineteenth century and was a hodge-podge of nature lore, moral fables and often light-hearted verse.

Early American children's books tended to follow the British pattern and, until the mid-nineteenth century, followed two distinct trends. The first consisted of the direct import of English books, while the second consisted of the educational, religious and ethical concepts embodied in Anglo-Saxon culture and traditions and expressed in early books written and published in the Colonial period. At least fifty years elapsed after the emergence of the United States as a separate political entity before any expression of a distinctive American way of life began to permeate children's books. In the seventeenth and eighteenth centuries American books aimed at the young were, in fact, often more extreme in their high-minded moralizing than their English counterparts. One of the earliest examples was John Cotton's *Spiritual Milk Drawn out of the Breasts of Both Testaments, chiefly for the Spiritual Nourishment of Boston Babes in either England,* published in 1646. The text, which was as high-flown and verbose as its title implies, was a model for many later works, culminating in the *New England Primer* of 1690. The formula of practical education mingled with religious precepts was varied only by grim and sombre story books.

Fairy tales

Side by side with the printed books aimed at the children of the upper and middle classes was a wealth of vernacular folklore preserved in the oral traditions of the lower classes. This peasant mythology was worldwide and the elements and themes of English, German or Scandinavian fairy tales may be traced in the folklore of India or China. Occasional glimpses of this world of fairies, giants, hobgoblins, trolls and elfs may be found in adult literature from Chaucer to Shakespeare, but there was no serious attempt to collect and set down these fairy tales until the late seventeenth century. The earliest printed versions of fairy tales appeared in Britain after the Restoration in 1660 and were the seventeenth-century equivalent of the late-Victorian 'penny dreadfuls'. These crudely printed little chapbooks, which were illustrated with simple woodcuts, improved dramatically in the early eighteenth century, largely as the result of the efforts of John Newbery.

Perrault's *Histoires ou contes du temps passé,* first published in 1697, crossed the English Channel some thirty years later and appeared under the title of *Histories, or Tales of past Times.* This ran to innumerable editions and established the standards for all subsequent books of fairy stories. Children's literature was transformed by John Newbery who not only put fairy tales on a firm footing but also established that brand of juvenile literature popularly known as toy books (see below). Newbery published one of the earliest collections of nursery rhymes, hitherto confined to occasional pieces, in *Tommy Thumb's Pretty Song Book* (*c.* 1744). The year 1760 was a particularly industrious one for Newbery, who produced three best-selling titles – *The Top Book of All, Mother Goose's Melody* and *Gammer Gurton's Garland.*

These rhymes and fairy tales combined the whimsical with the incredible and set the pattern for the light reading of children in Britain and America for almost a century. Fairy tales did not assume a more serious role until the 1820s when their ethnographical and sociological significance began to emerge. The systematic study and collection of popular mythology began with the Grimm brothers in Germany, and in 1823 the first volume of their fairy tales was published in English under the title *German Popular Stories,* with illustrations by George Cruikshank. Although Grimms' fairy tales, allied to the earlier fables of Perrault, remained paramount throughout the rest of the century, and are the foremost favourites to this day, they triggered off a fashion for the more serious fairy story and a vast literature developed in the second half of the century, drawing on the folklore and mythology of Greece and Rome, the Arthurian legends, the Norse sagas and other disparate sources. The ethnological approach culminated in the publication of a series of books of fairy stories, each volume designated by a different colour. These books, edited by Andrew Lang, with their elegant black-and-white drawings and full-colour plates in the

Miniature bookcases: The Child's Book-case and The Scientific Library

Right Prize edition of *The Pilgrim's Progress, c.* 1890

Above Frontispiece by Cruikshank for *Cinderella and the Glass Slipper,* 1853

manner of the Pre-Raphaelites, enjoyed a certain vogue at the turn of the century and remained popular into the 30s.

In the *Kjøbenhavns-Posten* for 17 March 1829 appeared 'The Snow Queen', the first of the fairy stories by Hans Christian Andersen. Six years later he published a booklet of sixty-four pages containing 'The Tinder Box', 'Little Claus and Big Claus', 'The Princess and the Pea' and 'Little Ida's Flowers'. Two similar volumes appeared in 1835–7 and numerous other parts, later published in omnibus volumes, were produced throughout the century. Andersen's fairy tales first appeared in England in 1846, in which year five volumes of his stories were published, including *Wonderful Stories for Children,* translated by Mary Howitt, and *A Danish Story-Book,* by Charles Boner.

Moral tales

The Puritanical approach to children's literature continued well into the twentieth century. To the purely religious aspects of the seventeenth century were added philosophical and even political overtones. Thus Thomas Day's *Sandford and Merton,* which went through three major editions between 1783 and 1789, incorporated the doctrines of Rousseau disguised as fairy tales. Maria Edgeworth was the most prolific writer of children's books with a strong socio-political theme which enjoyed a wide popularity in Britain and America in the late eighteenth century. Religious propagandists, like the Quaker social reformer Priscilla Wakefield, used children's stories to combat the social evils of her day. Mrs Trimmer's *Fabulous Histories,* published by Longmans in 1786, attempted to counter the purely frivolous elements of fairy tales while, at the same time, producing a book which would uphold the tenets of religion against the spread of revolutionary tendencies from France.

Stories of a more general, 'improving' nature developed early in the nineteenth century. Mary Martha Sherwood's *Fairchild Family* (1818) is a splendid example of the Calvinistic approach to moral tales, so typical of many of the books published throughout the nineteenth century. Many writers, now largely forgotten, went further and produced pious books interpreting everyday religious experience. These books complemented the purely religious aspects of the Sunday School movement which developed in the English-speaking world at this time. The best of these writers were the English Noncomformists Ann and Jane Taylor (best-remembered for 'Twinkle, twinkle little star') and Elizabeth Turner. On the other side of the Atlantic the Sunday School libraries were kept well supplied with the prolific writings of Catharine Maria Sedgwick, Susan Warner and Mrs S. J. Hale (the last-name immortalized by her rhyme 'Mary had a little lamb'). Mary and Charles Lamb, with their *Tales from Shakespear* (1807), combined the didactic with the moral element. Even in the so-called humorous works of the early nineteenth century the desire to teach, improve, warn and rebuke was ever present. Stories about naughty children who came to a sticky end began with Heinrich Hoffmann's *Struwwelpeter,* translated into English in 1848. In the second half of the century the social consciences of the young were pricked by Charles Kingsley's *Water Babies* (1863), enjoyed as a story to this day, long after the abuses of child labour, which it attacked, have been eliminated.

Many books originally aimed at adult readers subsequently became children's classics, enjoyed as good stories in which the moral element (important at the time of first publication) is of less significance. From Jonathan Swift's *Gulliver's Travels* (1726) to the novels of Charles Dickens, the adult fiction of one generation has tended to become the children's literature of the next—right down to George Orwell's *Animal Farm* (1945), which was enjoyed as a children's story and a savage political satire simultaneously.

Toy books

The crude chapbooks of the seventeenth and eighteenth centuries were the forerunners of the 'pretty gilt toys for girls and boys', as John Newbery described the light juvenile fiction which he launched in 1744 with *The Little Pretty Pocket-Book.* These books were strongly bound with gaily coloured Dutch-paper bindings, well printed and reasonably well illustrated. In content they avoided the strong moralizing so common at that time and were tolerably well written. They set the tone for similar toy books over the ensuing century.

Toy books entered a new era in 1864, when the London publisher Routledge

The windmill's made
to grind the corn,

The huntsman sounds
the bugle horn.

The captain boldly
draws his sword,

The crown becomes
Our sovereign lord.

The Trifler; or, Pretty Plaything, chapbook published London, *c.* 1840

commissioned the twenty-year-old artist Walter Crane to illustrate a series of eight-page toy books using a maximum of three colours. Over the ensuing decade Crane designed some thirty-eight toy books in the series, ranging from pictorial alphabets and nursery rhymes to the rather ambitious *Multiplication Table in Verse*. In 1877 Crane and the engraver Edmund Evans embarked on a much more ambitious series, from *The Baby's Opera* to *The Baby's Own Aesop* (1887), running to fifty-six pages each and priced at five shillings. From 1885 onwards he also produced the illustrations for a series of toy books published by Marcus Ward. Although these late Victorian toy books had no artistic pretensions at the time, they have since become important collectors' pieces. Subsequent artists whose work was reproduced in toy books of the late nineteenth century included Randolph Caldecott and Kate Greenaway, Thomas Crane (Walter's elder brother), Richard Doyle and Harrison Weir. These nineteenth-century toy books are all but forgotten today by children, though they possess enormous appeal for collectors. From the beginning of the present century the animal books of Beatrix Potter and the *Little Black Sambo* stories have remained perennial favourites.

Many of the toy books produced from the late nineteenth century made up for a lack of artistry by their novelty. Books with movable pictures date from about 1810, while those with 'stand-up' pictures date from the middle of the century. Odd-shaped books and panoramic books developed in the 1860s. The more robust books, printed on laminated boards, and the popular rag books pioneered by Dean, date from the early 1900s. Musical picture books and puzzle picture books both developed in the Edwardian period, and those with a three-dimensional effect created by an anaglyphic process, viewed with special red and green spectacles, began to appear in the 20s.

Towards the end of the century, however, the illustration of children's books became more sophisticated and was consciously influenced by the prevailing trends in art. Particularly noteworthy were the illustrations by H. J. Ford for the Lang series of Fairy Books. Much sought after are the early editions of Laurence Housman's stories accompanied by his own illustrations. At the beginning of this century H. R. Millar emulated Ford in the ethereal Art Nouveau style of his fairy-tale drawings and his illustrations for some of the later Kipling stories. Arthur Rackham's distinctive style became famous overnight with his illustrations for *Grimms' Fairy Tales* (1900). From then onwards he dominated children's book illustration of the early twentieth century, from *Rip Van Winkle* (1905) and *Gulliver's Travels* (1909) to *The Wind in the Willows* (1940), which appeared some months after his death. Sumptuous editions of these children's classics of the Edwardian era and the 20s are among the most sought after of modern children's books. Other artists of this period whose work is now increasing in value include Ernest Shepard, who illustrated *Winnie-the-Pooh* (1926), *The House at Pooh Corner* (1928), *The Golden Age* (1928) and *The Wind in the Willows* (1931); Kay Nielsen, *In Powder and Crinoline: Old Fairy Tales* (1913); and Edmund Dulac, whose best-known work

Opposite Illustration by Thomas Crane for *Abroad*, published by Marcus Ward, 1882

126

CHILDREN are happy with "Sister" all day,
Mothers can't nurse them—they work far away.
Good Sister Rosalie, she is so kind,
E'en when they're troublesome, she doesn't mind.
Here in the first room the Babies we see, sitting at *dejeuner* round Rosalie.

Dodo is crying, he can't find his spoon—some one will find it and comfort him soon.
Over yon cradle bends kind Sister Claire,
Dear little Mimi is waking up there.
Sister Félicité, sweetly sings she,
"Up again, down again, *Bébé*, to me."

W. Heath Robinson's
illustration for Bluebeard
from *Old Time Stories Told
by Master Charles Perrault*,
Constable & Co. Ltd,
London, 1921

is to be found in *The Arabian Nights* (1907), *Stories from Hans Andersen* (1911), *Edmund Dulac's Fairy-Book* (1916) and *Treasure Island* (1927).

Children's classics

The reaction against moral tales and the didactic element in children's stories began in the late 1830s with the publication of Catherine Sinclair's *Holiday House*, which positively condoned naughtiness, and with Edward Lear's *Book of Nonsense* (1846), which established a style of fantasy and surrealism which endures to this day. This paved the way for *Alice's Adventures in Wonderland*

(1865) and *Through the Looking-glass* (1872), which combined the talents of Lewis Carroll (the Rev. C. L. Dodgson) and the illustrator Sir John Tenniel. In the same genre were the *Golliwogg* books of Florence Upton, J. M. Barrie's *Peter Pan* (1904) and Kenneth Grahame's *The Wind in the Willows* (1908).

In America the best children's books were distinguished by their realism, beginning with the works of Nathaniel Hawthorne, from *Grandfather's Chair* (1841) to *Tanglewood Tales* (1853). Joel Chandler Harris produced, in his Uncle Remus tales, a worthy successor to Aesop's *Fables*. Some of the most perceptive writing about adolescent children appeared in the novels of Louisa M. Alcott, whose *Little Women* first appeared in 1868. Among the more notable European classics translated into English were Wilhelm Busch's *Max and Moritz* (1865), *The Swiss Family Robinson* of J. R. Wyss (1813), *Heidi* by Johanna Spyri (1881) and *Pinocchio* by Carlo Collodi (1882).

Just So Stories by Rudyard Kipling with cover designed by the author, 1902

Adventure stories

The hearty school of boys' writers began with Captain Frederick Marryat, whose adventure stories, *Peter Simple*, *Mr Midshipman Easy*, *Masterman Ready* and *The Children of the New Forest* (1834–47), are widely read to this day. The lure of far-away places provided the formula for such best-sellers as R. M. Ballantyne's *Coral Island* (1858) and R. L. Stevenson's *Treasure Island* (1883). James Fenimore Cooper's 'Leather-stocking' series began with *The Last of the Mohicans* in 1826 and continued with *The Pathfinder* and *The Deerslayer* (1840–1). The robust, homespun qualities of these books established the tradition followed by subsequent American writers who drew on first-hand experiences in the Civil War and the Wild West, from D. P. Thompson's *Green Mountain Boys* (1839) and *The Scalp Hunters* (1851) by Thomas Mayne Reid to E. Eggleston's *Hoosier School-Boy* (1883) and H. H. Jackson's *Nelly's Silver Mine* (1878).

G. A. Henty's adventure stories, set against historical backgrounds that ranged from the Tudor period to the Boer War, were in a class of their own and the original editions, with their distinctive pictorial bindings, are highly prized collectors' items today. Henty established the fashion for a robust brand of historical fiction which was subsequently developed by such writers as Herbert Strang, Percy Westerman and W. E. Johns, whose yarns span the period of the Second World War.

School stories

A curious facet of children's literature, particularly in Britain, is the fascination for stories based on life at boarding schools. This category probably started with the still-popular classic, *Tom Brown's Schooldays* by Thomas Hughes (1857) and Dean Farrar's mawkish moral tale of *Eric; or, Little by Little* (1858), but it was well established by 1882 when F. Anstey published his fantasy *Vice Versa: A*

Lesson to Fathers. The late nineteenth century witnessed the birth of lengthy school serials which had their heyday in the years between the World Wars, when St Dominic's, Greyfriars, St Austin's, the Manor House School and St Cyprian's were better known to countless readers than Eton and Harrow.

Penny dreadfuls, bloods and comics

The more ephemeral literature of the nineteenth century consisted of lurid paperbacks, the nickel and dime novels of America and the 'penny dreadfuls' or 'bloods' of Britain. Many of them pirated the ideas and characters of more reputable authors, and a considerable library could be formed of cheap novelettes which plagiarized Charles Dickens at the height of his popularity. The majority of the penny dreadfuls consisted of short stories and racy yarns of high adventure, whose heroes were distinguished more for brawn than brain and whose incredible deeds foreshadowed the twentieth-century exploits of Superman, Captain Marvel and others of the same breed. Most pulp literature of this class was execrably written and poorly printed; never intended to be kept, these books are of the greatest rarity nowadays and their antiquarian interest was not recognized till long after most of them had been thrown away.

Light-hearted periodicals for adolescent readers began to appear in the second half of the nineteenth century, emulating the success and the style of such adult magazines as *Punch*, which had been founded in 1841. Not surprisingly, one of the first of these imitators was named *Judy*, established in 1867, and though much of its humour seems infantile by modern standards, its editors deserve credit for some attempts to maintain high standards of text and illustrations in a field which was not generally noted for quality. One of *Judy's* more memorable characters was Ally Sloper, who was eventually promoted to having a comic paper of his own, entitled *Ally Sloper's Half Holiday*. The longest running of the Victorian comics was *Fun*, established in 1861 and closing down in 1901. Its editor Thomas Hood, son of the poet and humorist, also produced *Tom Hood's Comic Annual* from 1867 onwards. Several other annuals were published in the late nineteenth century and have preserved, in more permanent form, many of the droll characters who delighted Victorian children with their antics. The 90s was the era of the cheap comic, paralleling the tabloid newspapers of the period. The best-known of these juvenile papers were *Chips* and *Comic Cuts,* which established the strip cartoon as the narrative medium, complete with such artifices as balloon dialogue and a wide vocabulary of onomatopoeic expressions to convey both sounds and emotions.

It must not be imagined that children's periodicals were the monopoly of the vulgar and the trivial. A number of weekly magazines of an 'improving' nature were launched in the latter half of the century to combat the frivolity of comics. One of the first periodicals of this type was *Chatterbox*, founded in 1866, containing a miscellany of stories, articles, poetry and good illustrations. Two years later *Good Words for the Young* was launched; as its name implies, its high

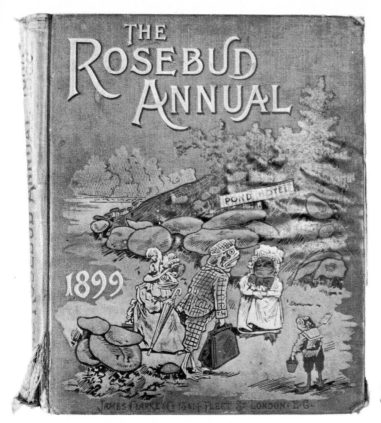

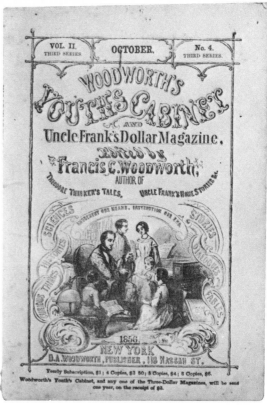

moral tone was evident in every page, but it provided wholesome entertainment none the less. *Little Folks* (1871) was aimed at the younger reader, while more specialized reading was provided by the *Boy's Own Paper* (1879) and the *Girl's Own Paper* launched the following year, both surviving well into the present century and providing serials by the best children's writers of the day, informative articles on every conceivable topic and practical hints on hobbies and pastimes.

In the 1890s the penny dreadful was transformed into the weekly paper containing serialized adventure and school stories of a generally higher standard than the 'bloods'. These papers, known today as Old Boys' Books, began with *Chums* (1892) and *The Captain* (1899), and by the time of the First World War there was a veritable galaxy of them, including *Union Jack*, *The Gem* and *The Magnet*. Within their pages appeared juvenile fiction ranging from school stories and westerns to spy stories and detective stories. Some of the more memorable characters featured in these papers ended up with regular periodicals of their own, such as *Greyfriars*, devoted to Frank Richards' tales of Billy Bunter and his schoolmates, or *Sexton Blake*, dealing with the exploits of the celebrated private detective. The tradition of these periodicals continues to this day in such comics as *Rover*, *Wizard*, *Adventure*, *Knockout*, *Dandy* and *Beano*, but such is the nostalgia for the Old Boys' Books of the turn of the century that many of them have been reprinted in recent years or distilled into anthologies.

Left The Rosebud Annual, 1899

Above Cover of Woodworth's *Youth's Cabinet,* New York, 1856

Pages from Dean's *Moveable ABC*, mid-19th century

For the true collector, however, there can be no substitute for the original and some remarkable prices have been paid for copies of *The Gem* and *The Magnet*, especially lengthy runs of these magazines.

From the collector's viewpoint the same holds good for nursery literature in general. Though many Victorian works have become standard classics which are still in print and have been translated into many languages, the chief interest lies in the early editions. For years children's books were completely overlooked by serious bibliophiles and it is only since the Second World War that the value of these items has been appreciated. Children's books and periodicals were subjected to hard usage and the collector who would spurn an adult book of the same period in less than pristine condition is forced to accept that where nursery literature is concerned condition is a relative term. Purely educational books are still an unconsidered field and there is scope for the collector in the ABCs, primers, copy-books and school textbooks of the Victorian era, which can often be picked up quite cheaply in second-hand bookshops and bookstalls.

132

Museums and Collections to Visit

Great Britain

Abbey House Museum, Leeds
Arreton Manor, Arreton, Isle of Wight
Aston Hall, Birmingham
Bethnal Green Museum, London
Birmingham City Museum & Art Gallery
Blaise Castle House Museum, Bristol
Bowes Museum, Barnard Castle
Cambridge & County Folk Museum
Castle Museum, York
Cornish Museum, Looe
Doll Museum, Warwick
Dumfries Museum, Dumfries
Grange Art Gallery & Museum, Brighton
Grosvenor Museum, Chester
Hereford City Museum & Art Gallery
Luton Museum & Art Gallery, Luton
Museum of Childhood, Edinburgh
Museum of Childhood, Menai Bridge
Museum of Childhood, Sudbury,
    Derbyshire
Museum of Childhood & Costume,
    Blithfield
Museum of Costume, Bath
North of England Open Air Museum,
    Beamish
Nostell Priory, Wakefield
Penrhyn Castle, Bangor
Platt Hall Gallery of English Costume,
    Manchester
Playthings Past Museum, Beaconwood, nr
    Bromsgrove
Pollock's Toy Museum, London
Preston Hall Museum, Stockton-on-Tees
Red House Museum & Art Gallery,
    Christchurch
Rotunda (The), Oxford
Saffron Walden Museum, Saffron Walden
Stangers' Hall, Norwich
Stroud Museum, Stroud
Tollcross Museum, Glasgow
Tunbridge Wells Museum & Art Gallery
Uppark, nr Petersfield
Wallington Hall, Cambo
Welsh Folk Museum, St Fagans
Worthing Museum & Art Gallery,
    Worthing

United States

Denver Art Museum, Colorado
Greenfield Village & Henry Ford Museum,
    Dearborn, Michigan
Hammond-Harwood House, Annapolis,
    Maryland
Henry Francis du Pont Winterthur
    Museum, Delaware
Metropolitan Museum of Art, New York
Museum of City of New York, New York
Old Sturbridge Village, Massachussets
Roger Morris-Jumel Mansion, New York
Shelburne Museum, Vermont
Society for the Preservation of New
    England Antiquities, Boston, Massachussets
Sunnyside, Tarrytown, New York
Wilcox House, Maine

Canada

Bowmanville Museum, Bowmanville,
    Ontario
Bytown Museum, Ottawa, Ontario
Cornell Hill Museum, Stanbridge East,
    Quebec
Dundas Museum, Dundas, Ontario
Grey Owen Sound Museum, Owen Sound,
    Ontario
Guelph Civic Museum, Guelph Peninsula,
    Ontario
London Public Library, London, Ontario
Percy Band Collection, Black Creek Pioneer
    Village, Toronto
Peterborough Centennial Museum,
    Peterborough, Ontario
Prairie Panorama Museum, Czar, Alberta
St Edmunds Township Museum,
    Tobermory, Ontario
United Counties Museum, Cornwall,
    Ontario
Yarmouth County Historical Society
    Museum, Yarmouth, Nova Scotia

Acknowledgments

The author and publishers would like to thank Mrs Rosemary L. Klein for undertaking the picture research in the United States. They would also like to thank the following museums, collections and photographers by whose courtesy the illustrations in the book are reproduced:

Barnes Museum of Cinematography 102 *left*
Birmingham Museums and Art Gallery (Pinto Collection) 41
Castle Museum, York 4-5, 57, 67 *bottom*, 77, 84 *bottom*, 92, 96, 102 *right*, 104 *bottom*, 106, 108, 109, 124 *right*, 131 *left*, 132
City Museums, Stoke-on-Trent 21 *top left*
Constable & Co. Ltd 128
Florida State University (Shaw Collection) 131 *right*
Fox Photos 100
Louis H. Frohman **17, 87**
Collections of Greenfield Village and the Henry Ford Museum, Dearborn, Michigan 13, 28, 63, 76, 111 *bottom*
Hammond-Harwood House, Annapolis, Maryland **69**
London Museum 99
The Metropolitan Museum of Art (The Sylmans Collection, Gift of George Coe Graves, 1930) 84 *top*
Museum of Childhood, Edinburgh 111 *top*, 120, 129
Museum of Childhood, Menai Bridge (photographs Angelo Hornak) 4 *left*, 16, 23, 34 *both*, 38, 40, 94
Museum of the City of New York 1, 3 *top* (The Byron Collection), 4 *bottom*, 5 *bottom*, 24, 27 *left*, 29 *top*, 39, 48, 55, 60 *top*, 62, 85, 107
Museum of English Rural Life, University of Reading 12
Milton Bradley Company 68, 101
National Museum of Wales (Welsh Folk Museum) 71, 112, 117

The National Trust **jacket** (The Nursery at Wallington Hall), 10, 78
New-York Historical Society, New York City 21 *top right* (Dauer Collection), 54
Old Sturbridge Village, Massachussets 74
Parker Brothers Games 73, 75
Philadelphia Museum of Art 14 *left* (Geesey Collection), 118 *bottom*
Phillips Auctioneers, London 30, 31 *bottom left and right*, 58, 60 *bottom*, 90, 113, 119
George Rainbird Ltd 3 *bottom left*, 128
John Rainsville 127
Red House Museum and Art Gallery, Christchurch (photographs Angelo Hornak) **18, 36, 70, 88**
Shelburne Museum Inc., Shelburne, Vermont 31 *top*, 46 *left*
Sheila Sherwen 3 *bottom right*
Edwin Smith 102 *left*, 104 *top*
Society for the Preservation of New England Antiquities 19
Sotheby's Belgravia 14 *right*, 33, 66, 91
Sotheby's Bond Street 14 *top*
Stroud Museum (photograph Angelo Hornak) **35**
Victoria and Albert Museum (Crown Copyright) 21 *bottom*, 26, 27 *right*, 29 *bottom*, 42, 45, 46 *right*, 47, 49, 50 *both*, 51 *both*, 52, 53, 64, 67 *top*, 80 *top and bottom right*, 82, 89, 93, 114 *both*, 115, 118 *top left and right*, 123, 124 *left*, 125
The Henry Francis du Pont Winterthur Museum 80 *bottom left*

Index